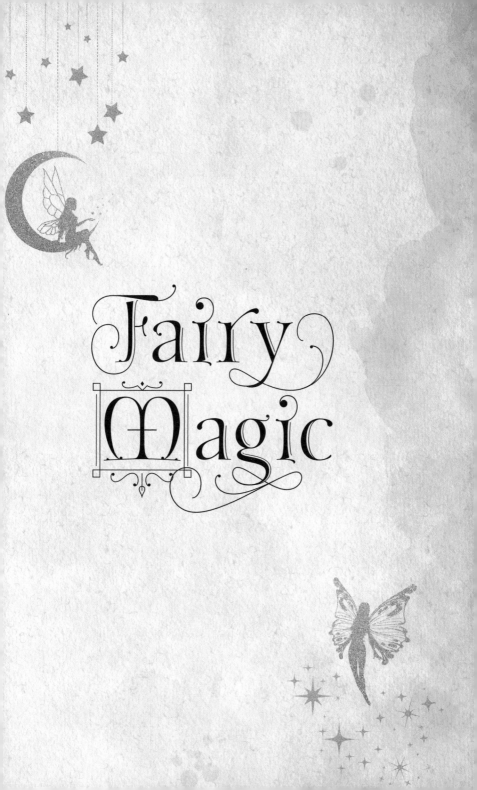

Fairy Magic

Fairy Magic

A Handbook of
ENCHANTING SPELLS,
CHARMS, *and* RITUALS

AURORA KANE

WELLFLEET
PRESS

Brimming with creative inspiration, how-to projects, and useful information to enrich your everyday life, quarto.com is a favorite destination for those pursuing their interests and passions.

© 2022 Quarto Publishing Group USA Inc.

First published in 2022 by Wellfleet Press,
an imprint of The Quarto Group,
142 West 36th Street, 4th Floor | New York, NY 10018, USA
T (212) 779-4972 F (212) 779-6058 www.Quarto.com

Wellfleet titles are also available at discount for retail, wholesale, promotional, and bulk purchase. For details, contact the Special Sales Manager by email at specialsales@quarto.com or by mail at The Quarto Group, Attn: Special Sales Manager, 100 Cummings Center Suite 265D, Beverly, MA 01915 USA

10 9 8 7 6 5 4 3 2 1

ISBN: 978-1-57715-243-9

Library of Congress Control Number: 2021946404

Publisher: Rage Kindelsperger
Creative Director: Laura Drew
Managing Editor: Cara Donaldson
Editors: Leeann Moreau and Elizabeth You
Cover & Interior Design: Emma Clayton
Layout Design: Sydney Martenis

Printed in China

For Brady and Landon, whose wonder-filled child's world is the secret place of the fairies

Contents

Introduction – 10

13

BELIEF TAKES FLIGHT

Origins of the Magical Fairy – 13

A Fairy Primer – 16

Fairies and Their Magical Powers – 20

Beware Malevolent Fairies – 24

The Fairy Realm – 26

The Fairy Portal – 26

Fairies as Spirit Guides – 29

33

MAKING THE FAIRIES' ACQUAINTANCE

Fairy Offerings for Friendship – 34

Tuatha Dé Danann – 38

Elementals and Nature Fairies – 42

Household and Helper Fairies – 66

Other Fairies: Angelic Fairies, Pranksters, and Trouble – 72

85

COMMUNICATING
WITH THE FAIRIES

Fairy Communication Etiquette – 86
Communicating and Working with the Fairies – 88
Planning a Fairy Garden – 94
Planting and Tending a Fairy Garden—Flowers,
Herbs, and Trees – 96
Magical Fairy Tools – 100

119

CREATE ENCHANTMENT
IN YOUR LIFE

Fairy Festivities – 120
Fairy Potions – 126
Fairy Meditations – 132
Fairy Spells and Rituals – 138

Epilogue – 171
Resources and References – 172
Index – 174
Acknowledgments – 176

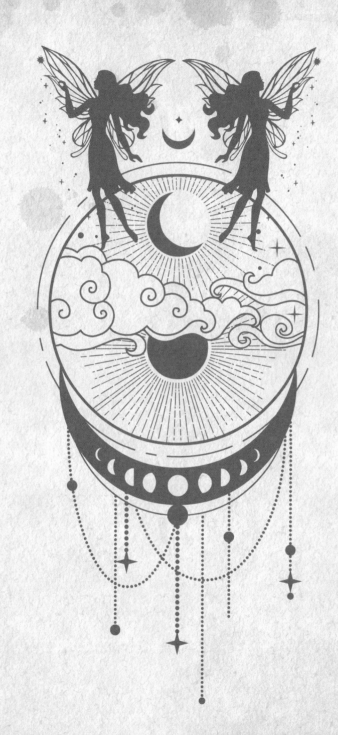

Of ancient lore and fairy facts this magic kingdom's built.
All entered here must truly be of purest mind and heart.

For good to come and love to grow, a fairy's dust imparts
the kind of magic you can share when manifesting starts.

Seek pixies, gnomes, an elf or two, and unicorns to ride
along this well-worn path to find where fairies really hide.

Bring trinkets, string, some cheese, and ale—
for good as gold they be
to soothe a fairy temper, they're intended to appease.

And what enchantment waits for you along this fairy path?
The knowledge that you seek to charm
the fairies to your side—a dance or two to celebrate the
magic that's inside.

We're off to meet the fairies now—adventure does await—
a pot of gold, a fairy stone, a magic garden gate.
Imaginary friends you've known may reappear this day,
for fairy's love begins at birth and never fades away.

May these pages read,
their glitter spread,
and fill your soul with joy.

Introduction

Welcome to the land of fairy magic—a place of joy, sparkle, romance, creativity, mystery, and miracle. For those who believe, when fairies take up residence in your heart, home, or garden, it becomes a truly enchanting space.

Fairies dwell everywhere among us—inhabiting marshes, forests, gardens, fields, ponds, lakes, rivers, and, sometimes, our homes— and are the special guardian keepers of all flowers everywhere. They are stewards of Nature and thrive among like-minded people. Though often hard to see, they adore interacting with animals and humans and are attracted to all things shiny. A fairy's presence is more likely felt than seen, but you may be among the lucky believers granted a glimpse into their fairy kingdom. The true of heart who keep childhood wonder alive in their soul are the most likely to be granted this privilege.

The benefits of inviting fairies into your magical life are many: They are uplifting spirits who will not abide a negative environment—whether from clutter, noise, pesticides, pollution, anger, or any other unhappy condition. Their upbeat attitude is a welcome antidote to the blues we all experience now and then. Fairies love *love* and scatter their charming fairy dust in honor and in search of it. Their joyous ways inspire creativity wherever they land. They nurture abundance, luck, and courage. Fairies practice herbal lore and healing and use their wisdom prudently. They boost spellwork with their favors granted and work on your behalf to manifest true intentions. Where fairies abide, so does

beauty, grace, and peace—not to mention that extra magical little something they lend to everything they do.

Most who practice magic embrace fairy magic as an element of delight and a way to connect to Nature and honor her seasons. Incorporating fairies into your magical practice is fun and easy—use all the tools you normally would, particularly natural ones, such as crystals, herbs, flowers, potions, and essential oils as well as the Moon's power, intuition, music, dance, meditation, journaling, and intention setting. Or create new ways to communicate with the benevolent beings that feel good to you. Or use only the beauty of your true heart—the most important tool for fairy magic. We'll explore these ideas and more in these fairy-dusted pages.

We'll also explore a little fairy history, discuss how to make the acquaintance of the fairies, tools to help with your fairy magic, uncover a little fairy lore, and then discover how best to work with the fairies, including some fairy spells, potions, and meditations to help you spread your honorary fairy wings.

Whether you're exploring the fairy kingdom because you're intrigued by these romantic beings or you wish to add another layer to your established magical practice, get ready to be enchanted.

Belief Takes Flight

F airy magic is found in the symbiotic relationships humans have with the supernatural, invisible spirit realm that exists parallel to our world—the land of the fairy kingdom. Fairy magic is for anyone who believes, though the fairies generally decide when they will cooperate and with whom they will work (hint: offerings help, but only when done with sincerity, and definitely not in payment). It is not a magic of complicated rituals but, rather, a magic of simplicity in opening yourself up to the wonder that can be glimpsed in the world by our subconscious and intuitive self. It is the help you need to navigate the world in a kinder, gentler fashion that leaves trails of hope and kindness wherever you've been. It is the magic of the heart combined with the magic of Nature. Don't worry, though, if your initial attempts at connecting with the fairies are met with resounding silence—listen more closely and don't give up.

ORIGINS OF THE MAGICAL FAIRY

The word "fairy" is derived from the Latin "fata," or goddess of fate, and the Old French word "faerie," meaning "enchantment." Known not to particularly care for the term, fairies prefer a number of other monikers, including Good People, Good Neighbor, Gentry, Themselves, Fair Folk, or Little People.

And, as the wee, or fae, folk are a mysterious lot, there seems to be some diversity of opinion on just where and when these supernatural beings originated. One such declaration says the earliest written documentation is in English literature, in *Otia Imperialia* by Gervase of Tilbury, a twelfth-century CE lawyer and scholar; another source cites Homer's *Iliad*, written much earlier, around the eighth century BCE, where he describes water fairies dancing. And ancient Greek myths told of fairy folk, too, in the form of Nymphs and Satyrs, and Roman tales of Genii, Lares, and Penates. Geoffrey of Monmouth introduced fairies into the tales of King Arthur in the twelfth century, Chaucer wrote of fairies in the fourteenth century, and Shakespeare gave us some of the most popular fairy creatures in *A Midsummer's Night Dream* in 1600.

Fairies have a presence everywhere among us and their powers are revered 'round the globe in all countries, cultures, and traditions, but their tales of origin and body of lore reign supreme in the countries of Great Britain—England, Scotland, and Wales, as well as Ireland, Germany, and Slavic and Nordic countries.

Although typically described as diminutive, winged creatures or green-clad jolly spirits that stay mostly invisible, the fairy kingdom is as varied as the human kingdom in appearance, size, personality, skill, likes, dislikes, and habitat preferences. Fairies tend to inhabit their spiritual form but sometimes reveal themselves, or are seen by those who believe. Most fairies are benevolent, but some are not—

it's important to protect yourself from those fairies who may wish to do you harm (more on that later). Fairies can be solitary sorts or gregarious, preferring to live in groups, villages, or other communities. All are playful and most love a good prank—and special powers abound.

There are numerous theories as to how fairies are born: Probably the most well-known theory (made famous by Tinker Bell), is that fairies are born from a baby's first laugh. Others believe they are actually fallen angels trapped on Earth. Some believe they are ghosts; others say they grow in cocoons along with the butterflies they adore. Nature fairies are thought to be ancestors of ancient Nature gods and goddesses. A widely held acceptance relates that fairies are descendants of the Tuatha Dé Danann (see page 38), or tribe of Danu—the great Celtic mother goddess and triple goddess—who were a godlike tribe possessing supernatural powers and who ruled Ireland by invasion nearly four thousand years ago. They themselves escaped invasion by turning invisible and fleeing into the vast hillside of Ireland to seek refuge, where they still reside today. Others think fairies just always "are" . . . a natural spirit of the world. And, although fairies are definitely *in* our world, they are definitely *not* of our world . . . existing almost on a parallel plane, which is what can make them so hard to find.

And, as the fairy population grew, so, too, did the number of "types" of fairies. Here, we'll learn about some of the many fairies populating the realms of elemental and Nature fairies, household, or helper, fairies, and other types of fairies, such as angelic fairies, the witty prankster fairies, and siren fairies.

A FAIRY PRIMER

T he fairies themselves seem to identify with certain types of populations, and many associate themselves with a specific element, such as air, fire, earth, water, etc., or identify with their environment, such as Flower Fairies, or Woodland Fairies. To take a quick glimpse into the many types of fairies you may encounter along your fairy magic journey, let's briefly consider some types,

INTERNATIONAL FAIRY DAY

June 24 is International Fairy Day, a day to celebrate these wee, wondrous, whimsical beings and recognize that these spritely spirits enchant and exist in almost every culture, with their reputation for good or evil, enchanting or not. June 24 falls during Midsummer week, a celebration of Midsummer Solstice and a time when the veil between our world and the fae is said to be thinnest. Fairy communication and activity are heightened . . . be vigilant at sunrise and sunset, when the fae are most likely about. And, however you choose to celebrate, include an offering of gratitude for the magical influence the fairies are in your life—but don't wait until next June 24 to do the same. Every day can be filled with the magic of the fae.

which we'll learn more about as we go. Keep in mind, though, that with so many fairy types, we'll just scratch the surface here. Lots of sources exist for more research on any of the fae folk who tempt you into their world.

- ALUX AND CHANEQUE: Nature fairies of Mexico; caretakers of the place in which they live

- ALVEN: a water fairy inhabiting the Elbe River who travels in bubbles along the water

- BEAN-SIDHE OR BANSHEE: an Irish/Scottish fairy who cries the wail of death

- BOGGART: a malicious household spirit, some say a Brownie gone bad, and perhaps the original "Bogeyman"

- BOGLE: an ill-tempered spirit, similar to a Goblin, who focuses its bad temper on those who deserve it

- BROWNIE: a helpful, benevolent Scottish household spirit

- CHANGELING: not exactly a fairy, but a fairy's child swapped for a human child

- CLURICHAUN: related to the Leprechaun, but whose job is to protect the home's wine stock

- DEVA: a Nature fairy . . . if you've ever seen a firefly, you've likely seen a Deva

- DRYAD: a tree and forest fairy

- DUENDE: Spanish house fairy

- DWARF: similar to a Gnome in appearance and habitat

- ELF: protector of the forest realm; with enchanting eyes and pointy ears, the Elf most closely resembles humans

- **ESPRIT FOLLET:** mischievous house fairy (a type of Bogle) similar in form and appearance to Will-o'-the-Wisp and in attitude to Puck, found in Northern France and who is very hard to rid oneself of once it takes up residence

- **GNOME:** shy, dwarf-like fairies who live among the tree roots and caves in the forest

- **GOBLIN:** generally describing a small, unattractive, malicious fairy; when prefaced with "hob," (such as Hobgoblin) the meaning changes to one less evil (beware the trick or two, though)

- **IRISH SEA WATER GUARDIANS:** tiny fairies who swim with the dolphins and fiercely protect the Irish Sea and her creatures

- **KELPIE:** dangerous water fairies, often appearing in the form of a horse: beware

- **KNOCKERS:** friendly mine fairies of Cornwall

- **KOBOLD:** a mine fairy from Germany

- **LEPRECHAUN:** a cobbler fairy

- **MERFOLK (MERMAIDS AND MERMEN):** beautiful, half human-half fish fairies who live underwater

- **NISSE:** Norwegian household spirit, like a Kobold or Brownie; called Tomte in Sweden

- **NYMPH:** beautiful, seductive Nature fairies who live among the trees, flowers, mountains, woods, and water; typically benevolent but sometimes mischievous

- PERIS: benevolent fairies of Persian lore

- PIXIE: your typical winged "fairy" fairy, who interacts with humans the most and makes themselves at home in many a garden

- POOKA: akin to Puck, a shape-shifting mercurial fairy whose good deeds or bad may be determined by whim

- REDCAP: a murderous fairy creature who inhabits castle ruins along the Scottish-English border

- SALAMANDER: associated with the element of fire; typically appear as fiery lizards and their passion burns bright . . . be careful of the heat

- SEELIE (BLESSED) COURT: the most beautiful of the fairies, they assemble at dusk to keep order and peace among the many fairy tribes

- SELKIE: a fairy able to transform from a seal into a human

- SPRITE: a type of Elf fairy of the element water, whose main job is to paint the leaves their vibrant colors each autumn

- SYLPH: a winged feminine spirit of the air whose messages are carried on the wind

- WILL-O'-THE-WISP: active at night and typically seen as light reflecting on water due to its fiery nature; look closely at the Moon's reflection in water to find the Will-o'-the-Wisp

- UNSEELIE (UNBLESSED) COURT: hoodlum fairies; the opposite of Seelie Court fairies

- YAKSHA: Nature fairy, of the Hindu and Buddhist traditions, with a split personality

- YOSEI: Japanese fairies, often spied as birds

FAIRIES AND THEIR MAGICAL POWERS

*A*ll fairies possess supernatural powers and magical abilities, but a fairy's individual powers vary based on the fairy type they belong to and their personality. And although fairies use their magical powers on and for humans (not always for good), fellow fae seem to be unaffected by them.

- ⌒ ANIMAL COMMUNICATION: Fairies love animals and establish especially close relationships with many, just like we do with our pets. The animals live among Nature, sharing the world with the fairies and developing a remarkable ability to communicate with them—in all the same ways as humans—especially by telepathy, which they can also apply to humans.

- ⌒ BRILLIANCE: In addition to the typical sparkle and glitter emitted by fairies, some are able to channel energy through their bodies into bright light, which can be hurled as a weapon or used to otherwise fend off threats.

- ⌒ CURSES: Though mainly a benevolent lot, fairies do have the gift of the curse—just as some witches do. So, stay on their good side to protect yourself from succumbing to enchanted sleep or being turned into a toad!

- ENHANCED SENSES: Fairies have the gift of enhanced senses, but especially clairsentience, the ability to sense invisible energy as a physical feeling, such as the goosebumps you get when walking past a cemetery, or the uplifting excitement, or draining sadness, you get from the energy in a room; and clairvoyance, the ability to see and sense into the future with your mind's eye.

- FLIGHT: Some fairies possess the ability to fly from place to place and some are so agile and quick they appear to fly.

- GLAMOUR: This fairy bewitchment causes things to appear much more beautiful than they are and not at all as they exist in the world. They are always illusions, conjured by temporary spells whose ends are unpredictable, and should never be requested for self-gain. Fairies may often use glamour as a means of distraction or survival. Wearing a four-leaf clover is said to give you a glimpse of the true fairy behind the disguise.

- GREEN THUMB: When fairies take up residence in your garden, you'll reap the benefits of their true connection with Nature. Their innate protective feelings toward Earth and all its inhabitants produce a supernatural ability to tend to plants of all kinds. Magnificent blooms, bean stalks growing to the sky, strongly scented plants and lush herbs, and abundant crops are gifts from the fairies.

- HEALING: Many fairies live among the healing herbs of Nature and use their healing energies to help humans.

INVISIBILITY: Most fairies are invisible—or move so quickly as to appear so—but may, if they feel safe, reveal themselves to you, though you may not immediately recognize what you're seeing! If your sense of clairvoyance is active, you may be able to see fairies around you on your own.

LONG-LIVED: Fairies do not age in the same way or at the same rate as humans. In fact, their lives are so long that many are believed to be immortal, but they can suffer injuries that can lead to death. When a fairy dies, their essence turns to glittering fairy dust to nourish the land, where it awaits rebirth among Nature's laughter.

LUCK: In return for a favor or agreed-upon outcome, the fairies may grant you the luck needed to achieve your wished-for dreams. Beware a broken agreement or ungrateful heart, as you may just as quickly find your luck take a turn for the worse.

MAGIC: Fairies are pure magic—and display many magical powers, such as granting wishes, making humans invisible, healing, and influencing luck. A good and grateful relationship with the fairies encourages them to use their magic on your behalf for good outcomes.

RESILIENCE: Fairies bounce back from trauma or injury much more quickly than humans and are able to take physical harm in larger amounts without the same ill effects humans feel.

↶ SHAPE-SHIFTING: Fairies have the supernatural ability to present themselves in whatever shape or form they desire (which also influences why you may not recognize them immediately). The shapes they favor include crows, magpies, and other black animals, especially when they're trying to deceive humans or lead them astray—be on guard!

MIDNIGHT—THE FAIRY HOUR

Beware midnight, the fairy hour, a time when trickster and malevolent fairies delight in leading humans astray, or worse, abducting them to Fairyland. It is also a time believed to obscure the fairies who wish to abduct human children, leaving changelings in their place.

BEWARE MALEVOLENT FAIRIES

Although the thought of fairies flitting about the Earth tends to make us smile and want to know them better, there are those whose evil ways you should avoid. The Scottish know them as the Unseelie Court (see page 81). Even the fairies you trust can turn on you if offended (easily) or feel ignored or taken for granted. Evidence of their wrath can be seen and felt in small things like unexplained pinching, tangled hair, milk that keeps souring, gardens that won't produce, terrible messes, or everyday items that go missing, and more harmful events such as ill health, kidnapping, or destructive weather. If you find yourself at the mercy of a seriously evil fairy—or unable to rid yourself from a less evil but still unwanted presence—try these time-proven remedies.

- IRON: Iron is the most powerful fairy repellent there is and believed to be one of a very few items that can actually kill a fairy—not something recommended, as the price of punishment could be severe. Fasten an iron bolt upon your door, carry a nail with you for protection, or follow the time-honored tradition of hanging an iron horseshoe—with iron nails for double protection—in your entryway.

- PLANT A ROWAN TREE: Tossing its red berries at the fairies or carrying a wand made from its wood are some of the best protectors from evil fairies. The tree itself, much feared by the fairies, will also protect your home.

- HERBAL REMEDIES: Carry St. John's wort, red verbena, daisies, or yarrow for its ability to repel fairies. Hang marsh marigold in the barn to keep the horses safe from the fairies' penchant for wild midnight rides.

- OFFERINGS: Soothe their tempers and stay in good favor
  with offerings of ale, bread, butter, cream, honey, or milk—but
  only as gifts, never in payment. See page 34 for more ideas
  on using offerings.

- SALT: Sprinkle liberally to establish a protective barrier
  anywhere you do not wish the fairies to roam—and especially in
  doorways and windowsills to stop them at points of entry. Salt
  any food you do not want stolen and toss some salt in the bath
  to establish a protective aura around yourself.

- To stay safe at night and avoid being Pixie-led (see page 77),
  wear your garments inside-out. This tactic is also said to save
  you, if captured by the fairies . . . it's worth a try, if need be!

- When on fairy turf, NEVER eat food offered by fairies—
  especially if you've been abducted by them, for you may never
  return home. That rule is a little less clear when the fairies
  bring gifts of food to you in your realm. Refusing to eat fairy
  foods, then, *may* result in retribution from the fairy folk for
  insulting them.

THE FAIRY REALM

So, where exactly will you find fairies? Where do they prefer to hang out and do their fairy business? Everywhere!

In the physical realms, the fairies are of the flowers, herbs, trees, forests, and meadows; the lakes, oceans, rivers, and streams; among the fauna; underground and aboveground. They are in the wind and the rain, the Sunlight and Moonlight; they are in fire and water and music and song. They dance among the stars and sing among the crickets.

In that parallel unseen realm, the fairies choose when and to whom they make themselves known. If you're ever in doubt of their presence, listen for the lullaby of the rain, the rebuke of thunder, the secrets whispered by the leaves, or the warning from a rose's thorn. Fairies and their magic are in our hopes and dreams, our acts of kindness and care. They are the spirits who lift ours in times of need. They are our angels on Earth and the kiss of the sky.

That said, like humans, fairies have their preferred habitats, and we'll learn more about those as we go along. With the heart and eyes of a child, you'll soon find your fairy magic companions.

THE FAIRY PORTAL

Entering the magical Fairy Realm—of your own accord and with the purest of intentions—is entering the world of possibility where space and time take on new meaning. It is a place to learn and grow and boost your magical energies and manifest your magical intentions. (Being taken there under duress is a different story, which we'll touch on at various points.) The solstice and equinox are prime times, as well as dusk and New Moons. Fairy lore gives us many ways to enter their Realm but there are two widely known ways to enter the fairy kingdom: by the fairy ring or the fairy door.

Should you spy a ring of mushrooms or stones, perhaps even flowers or grass, that marks a spot separated from others, you've likely stumbled upon a fairy ring. Entering the ring often means being transported to the beautiful fairy kingdom where magic and adventure await. If you're unsure, visit the site at dusk and listen for the sounds of music and laughter emanating from the fairy party typically held within the ring—then, you'll know for sure.

The other, the fairy door, can be found at the base of many a tree in the forest. With open mind and open heart, search the forest for that door. Let your intuition guide you. Learn to listen to the cues of the forest. When you perceive that the light, temperature, sounds, and smells have changed (and you may even feel as though you're being watched), look around you, for the fairy door is near. One must only knock gently three times and with true intentions to gain entry.

If there is no ring or door around, try these other ideas to enter the Realm of the Fairies, or at least signal that their company is desired—*but do take caution:*

- Nap under a hawthorn tree.

- Sip elderberry wine or elderflower liqueur under the elder tree.

- Swim under the Moon's full light.

- Watch the Sunlight sparkle on water.

- Gaze into a flickering flame.

- Follow the butterflies.

- Walk into the mist rising from the forest floor.

- Pick fresh strawberries at dawn and sip the dew left on their leaves.

- Seek the end of a rainbow.

- Listen to the song of the wind.

- Make or install your own fairy house or door inside or out.

FAIRIES AS SPIRIT GUIDES

*A*lthough fairies can be guilty of living in the moment and sometimes shirking responsibility, they are an intuitive bunch with tremendous insight into Nature and the world and working with its energies, as well as clairvoyant and clairsentient beings eager to use their knowledge for good. These complicated spirits have long been revered for their aid in healing and magical workings and have an undeniable role in bringing us messages from another realm.

As such, fairies, like spirit animals, often take responsibility to be our spirit guides—and, yes, they will choose you, not the other way around, though your magical aura is likely what caught their attention! As spirit guide, a fairy will deliver messages and lessons intended to guide, protect, inform, and impart wisdom. They know the path you should walk and will take your hand to lead you there. They will always work in your best interest, but that does not mean they will always see that you get what you want. Sometimes, what you *need* may be more important. They may stay with you as guides forever or only in certain situations, as you need.

You can communicate with your spirit fairy guide in the same way you'll learn to communicate with all the fairies in the fairy kingdom. Once you can sense your guide's presence, you may want to practice asking for specific advice. Keep your senses alive and be ready to receive their messages.

Though you may be able to sense their companionship through your physical senses, most often their guidance will come in the form of dreams, intuition, and visions or gut feelings. Pay attention when certain patterns start to appear repeatedly in your life—especially coincidences—they may have deep meaning from your spirit fairy guide. There is no end to the way spirit fairy guides may communicate with you. Take note, too, if you can, of the type of fairy guide you attract. That may have special meaning as well. For example:

- **Bean-sidhe or Banshee**, the wailing spirit who foretells death, may just be sending us a message to rid our lives of what no longer serves. Do not be frightened by her keening; she is here to warn and guide.

- **Elves**, these hardworking, hard playing spirits may be telling you to work harder or play harder, depending on your circumstances. Let them show you how.

- **Fire Fairies**, such as the Salamander, may represent a need to explore your more fiery side. Whatever your passion, with their help, you can achieve it. If you're hesitant to take risks or have trouble making decisions, a visit from a Salamander spirit guide could be just the fire you need lit underneath you to get moving. These spirits can help guide you through even the most difficult change.

- **Gnomes**, of the Earth, bring us messages of stability, protection, and nurturing. Any of the Earth fairies may suggest the need to develop a greater sense of grounding in your life, or may reward you with a jewel from the treasures of Earth's coffers as acknowledgment for your Nature stewardship—and will delight in your pleasure at receiving it.

- ᏋᏋ **Nature Fairies** may be bringing you a message of lightness. Smile, lighten up on yourself, celebrate your beauty and uniqueness, or spread joy wherever you can. They may also suggest that spending time in Nature is good for your soul. Follow their lead.

- ᏋᏋ **Pixies**, as more solitary fairies, bring a message of me-time and self-care. Heed their advice.

- ᏋᏋ **Sylphs**, or any of the air fairies, can be the winds of change and a breath of fresh air. They can signal it's time to take a deep breath and calm the mind and heart as well as bring messages from beyond or signal the need to listen to our intuition.

- ᏋᏋ **Undines**, water fairies such as the Mermaid, can guide in all situations regarding emotion, sensuality, transition and change, and intuition.

A genuine nod of appreciation for your spirit fairy guide's help is always appreciated as are gestures of kindness toward Nature and our fellow humans. If a gift feels right, make it honey.

Now that we know a bit more about the fairies, let's explore making their acquaintance.

Making The Fairies' Acquaintance

The fairies are a varied folk, and most fairies can be categorized in one or more categories. Don't worry, though, if you're not entirely sure of the correct category. Get to know them for their individuality and be grateful for their blessings.

A word of caution: meeting and getting to know the fairies is not as simple as just deciding it's what you want to do today. They can be a wary bunch, individually and collectively, and cultivating an honest relationship based on trust and openness is the first task—and this can take some time. There are lots of suggestions throughout this book for ways to start and further those special relationships, but a simple practice that will be good to establish is that of making fairy offerings.

FAIRY OFFERINGS FOR FRIENDSHIP

airies love gifts!—and making fairy offerings is your chance to extend an open invitation to the fae to join your life, to let them know you care, are interested in them, and are eager to get to know them. Offerings should be made with care and thought to what will please the fairies, as well as represent a part of you . . . so, some natural thing you've transformed, like making food or music, or even art to decorate your fairy altar or fairy garden (see pages 101 and 94). Offerings are also ways to express gratitude for the fairies' magical energies or any help they give you freely, and offerings should always be made from a generous heart. Fairy offerings are key to establishing relationships and building trust: consistency is key here, too.

There are numerous ideas for appropriate offerings to make as well as where to leave them. If you leave offerings anywhere other than on your own property, always ask permission from the property owner, if need be, and leave only natural offerings that are sure to do no harm to any plant or animal life (including humans) that may come upon them. If leaving offerings on your property, which is what I recommend, they can be left inside or out, close to where you'd like the fairies to enter your realm, but again, please do so safely and with the knowledge that what you leave will do no harm.

Know, too, that once you make the offering, you cannot take it back (or eat it later!). Plan on cleaning up anything the fae leave behind to prepare the space for your next offering.

Here are some suggestions to help you get started planning your offerings. Add what has meaning to you:

- BEER: in acorn caps for a quick sip, or poured directly onto the ground. (Those fairies love to party!)

- BIRDSEED: a double offering—the birds will be grateful, too, and you'll doubly impress the fairies by taking care of the birds.

- BREAD AND CAKE: note that this is not good for birds, so be selective about when and where you leave it.

- CLEAN WATER: in a larger container for sharing or in thimbles for individual fairy spa baths or sipping (before the bath, obviously!).

- CREAM AND BUTTER: fairy favorites.

- DRIED HERBS AND FLOWERS: in months when summer has passed.

- FALLEN LEAVES: write the fae a message on fallen leaves and leave sweet notes for them to find.

- FLOWER SEEDS: for the fairies to plant in their gardens.

༄ FRESH, ORGANIC BERRIES: preferably from your garden, but you can purchase them. Leave on a small cloth set up for a fairy picnic!

༄ HONEY: another fairy favorite—maybe even the most favorite!

༄ LAUGHTER: tell a joke!

༄ MUSIC: hang wind chimes, or sing or play an instrument.

༄ NATURE'S FOUND THINGS: collections of seashells, twigs, stones, pinecones, nuts, flower heads, or flower petals.

༄ RIBBON: just because it's pretty.

༄ SHINY THINGS: coins, crystals, eco-friendly glitter (see page 128), a gazing ball, glass, old jewelry, anything sparkly.

THE FAIRY TREE

*The hawthorn tree, often found standing alone in its environment,
is the legendary tree of the fairies—a place so sacred to them that
grave harm may befall any who deface it (which is why it's left
standing!). Portals to magical realms are said to exist beneath the
flowering hawthorn. Although its presence inside the house was
viewed as bad luck, a branch placed outside it, above the doorway,
warns evil spirits away and, as such, the hawthorn tree is a
common resident in a witch's garden.*

*When looking for a fairy tree, seek out the oldest specimens
as they have the most knowledge to impart. Rest your hand or your
back against its trunk and ask to speak to its fairy inhabitants.
Always seek permission before harvesting anything from the tree
and take care of the land on which it grows.*

*Two other important varieties of fairy tree include the oak and ash.
Spying all three trees together—hawthorn, oak, and ash—is called
the magical fairy tree triad, whose mere sighting is said to endow
you with the great good luck of the Irish fairies, and, perhaps, even
a glimpse into their world.*

TUATHA DÉ DANANN

Translating to "People of the Goddess Danu," the Tuatha Dé Danann are a mythical Celtic race of supernatural beings endowed with the gift of magic. Accounts of their ancestry, history, and existence vary. For our fairy magic purposes, let's consider their connection to the fae and history in that context.

Considered by some to be a noble court descended from the goddess Danu, they conquered Ireland from the Northern Isles and gave rise to the Irish fairies and elves. They, in turn, are said to descend from earlier Irish inhabitants, the Nemedians, forced to leave their homeland. On their return to Ireland, the Tuatha Dé Danann were renowned for their skills in magic, science and Nature, and healing. On arrival, legend says, they burned their ships, leaving no option for return and giving birth to the theory they arrived in the mist.

The Tuatha Dé Danann brought with them four magical treasures of the four cities—some say Otherworld—from whence they came:

- The *Stone of Fál*—the coronation stone of the kings of Ireland—that cried out in joy when stepped upon by a true king

- The magical *Spear of Lugh of the Silver Arm*, a.k.a. the Spear of Destiny, unbeatable in battle and which became a lightning bolt when thrown

- A powerful *Sword of Light*, from which no person ever escaped

- *Dagda's Cauldron*, able to feed all those who needed to be nourished from its unending bounty and heal those who drank its water—and perhaps even grant access to the Otherworld through its bottomless abundance

Despite their skills and treasures, however, the Tuatha Dé Danann were eventually overthrown by new invaders known as the Milesians. Forced now to flee their homeland, the Tuatha Dé Danann took refuge in the hills, valleys, and caves all over the Irish countryside, as they were forced to live out of sight or in exile (or perhaps they preferred not to surrender to these new conquerors!) and acquired a new name: People of the Fairy Mound, or the Sidhe Faerie Folk. These new fairy folk were not only revered for their great magical skills and willingness to help their neighbors, but also for their great beauty and courtly dress, which is said always to include some item of green. Contributing to their ability to stay out of sight were their powers of invisibility (acquired in a shroud of mist) and transformation, or shape-shifting.

The tunnels they dug all across Ireland enabled them to visit fairy villages near and far—each identified by the lone hawthorn tree marking the territory.

The fairies busied themselves in daily pursuit of similar occupations to the everyday Irish and their parallel world was envied for its great beauty, exquisite music, and unending joy.

Mortals transported to Fairyland were not always able to return home, or did so only after paying a penalty for their boorish behavior. Time passes differently there, too. Deliberate requests for entry or seeking entry portals are to be undertaken with extreme caution.

Don't expect the members of this elite fairy court to respond to your beck and call. You have much to learn before they'll consider you an ally.

DANU, FAIRY QUEEN

Danu means "flowing," and although in ancient Irish tradition she is thought to be the oldest of the Celtic goddesses, fair little is known about the fair Danu. Most famously, she is credited as being the mother of all Irish gods and people, including the fairy people—that disparate group of otherworldly magical folk she reunited and nurtured to great skill and strength. She is also sometimes referred to as their fairy queen. Her powers of leadership and natural inclination toward teaching are key to the survival of the Tuatha Dé Danann.

Danu brings us the comfort, love, and acceptance of a mother, the grounding of Earth, the wisdom of experience, the bounty of children and harvest, and the healing, soothing powers of water. No matter the challenge, Danu does not back down or give up.

The Sabbat festival of Beltane, May 1, or May Day, celebrates Danu, as spring's peak is about to burst into summer's abundance. Turn to her when you're in need of a reassuring embrace in today's tumultuous world.

ELEMENTALS AND NATURE FAIRIES

T hese delightful fairies are a basic categorization of fae folk corresponding with Nature's four elements: air, fire, earth, and water, which also exist within us and help connect us to the natural world, and the Nature fairies. These benevolent beings are a class of fairies who thrive among Nature, where they recharge their fairy energies used for tending plants, animals, land, sea, weather, humans, and more. Each elemental fairy has its own responsibilities among Nature. When they join forces, true magic ensues.

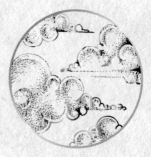

Air fairies, like pixies and angels, are the most common of the bunch . . . light and delicate, sprouting wings and spreading joy and good luck, sprinkled with a little fairy dust and fun along the way.

Their energies are of youth, creativity, communication, intuition, inspiration, intellect, tranquility, and travel.

Signs they're nearby include the tinkling of wind chimes or a melody from any bell-shaped flowers, an unexpected breeze, the chatter of leaves, a swaying of the flowers, buzzing of the bees, a sensed change in the weather, or a sense of movement in stillness.

Fire fairies, also called Salamanders, live in trees and old logs, making a hasty departure when one is cut down or tossed on the hearth. Though varying in appearance, they frequently resemble their lizardlike alternate name.

Fire fairies are of transformation, purification, passion, and energy. They can banish and reveal.

Signs they're nearby include the dancing of a candle's flame, a sudden increase in temperature, an unexplained glow or sparkle in the air.

Earth fairies, such as Gnomes and Elves, live deep in the Earth and may also frequent your garden. They have a deep respect for Earth and all its creatures and expect humans to adopt the same attitude.

Earth fairies tend to the physical world—its fertility, growth, strength, and health. They nourish and ground, spreading security, abundance, and permanence.

Signs they're nearby include an unexpected patch of disturbed earth, a sense or grounding and serenity, a sudden aroma of fresh earth or blooming plants, the sudden appearance of an animal, or a feeling of déjà vu.

Water fairies, like Merfolk and Sprites, are the most mysterious of the group. Usually benevolent in spirit, they avoid humans. Tending to their watery habitats, such as ponds, rivers, and oceans, can go a long way toward making friends with these marvelous creatures, who crave tranquility.

Water fairies are of cleansing, going with the flow, and honoring emotions. They are the fairies of dreams, relationships, change, cleansing, healing, hope, fluidity, and rebirth.

Signs they're nearby include ripples or brilliant reflections on water, morning dew drops, a sweet rain shower while the Sun shines, a sudden increase in humidity, or the sighting of a rainbow.

And, as the name implies, **Nature fairies** live among Nature—caring for Earth and all her elements and inhabitants. Flowers are a special project for fairies: Each flower has its own guardian fairy and it's believed that the fairy inhabits the personality of the plant. The Nature fairies are a merry, gentle lot that includes elementals, Flower Fairies, Tree Fairies, Gnomes, Elves, Pixies, Sprites, Merfolk, and even Unicorns. These fairies are mainly invisible—and most often first met as an "imaginary friend." Their world is one of laughter, sparkle, and love.

Nature fairies have supreme gifts of manifestation when the heart and goals align and are true. They're eager to help and oblige when asked.

Signs they're nearby include all of those listed for the elementals, as well as thriving plant life, intoxicating aromas, tidy and well-tended landscapes, remnants of fairy dust, and whatever your fairy intuition picks up along the way.

Let's get to know these fae folk a little better. Keep your eyes, ears, and sixth sense open along the way!

FAIRY CLASSES

Fairies from English, Irish, Scottish, and Welsh lore fall among two main classes: solitary and trooping. Solitary fairies, obviously enough, prefer their own company and to live alone, on their own, and tend to favor the trickster or troublesome personalities. Trooping fairies form "troops" and adore group activities, most notably the long fairy processions, called fairy rades, accompanied by the distinct jingling of fairy bells. This class comprises of kindly as well as unruly fairies. A third class, domesticated, has been proposed for household spirits and helper fairies. The Scottish, too, recognize the Seelie (blessed) and Unseelie (cursed) Courts. The Norse Elves are either light (good) or dark (evil).

ASRAI

British folklore brings us Asrai, a beautiful otherworldly fairy, similar to a Mermaid, who dwells deep underwater. She is a slender creature, clothed only in her long hair. The Asrai fears Sunlight, which can melt her into the water in which she lives, and she is nourished by the Moon's light. Asrai, though shy, surfaces once each century, and while beautiful to behold, do not be tempted to touch her, for her ice-cold touch in return means you will never feel warmth again.

AZIZA

A Nature spirit inhabiting the forest, the Aziza fairy comes to us through the West African folklore of the Dahomey People. These tiny fairies can offer spiritual guidance and the practical skills of survival in the forest. Helpful by nature, they easily offer aid to hunters and travelers and share their knowledge of working with fire for good. Their knowledge of healing herbs is gained from centuries of wise study. And although willing to spread their wisdom for the benefit of humans, Aziza can be hard to find, preferring the depths of the forest. If you're lucky enough to encounter them, you'll know they are there from the lovely glow they emit, and you may hear the soft beat of their wings as they flit by.

DEVA

An invisible Nature spirit, whose name means "shining one" in Sanskrit, the Devas come to us from a Hindu tradition of a type of enlightened, higher being almost akin to angels. Devas are everywhere, hovering around us as a sort of cloud of human subconsciousness since time existed. Humans with the keen senses of clairvoyance and clairaudience are able to detect Devas, catching a glimpse of their aura or a snatch of a tune—their messages are of help or warning. Devas are a busy lot, with one being assigned to every living thing. Their deep concern for Nature has formed the basis of a cooperation, of sorts, between Devas and humans to tend to Earth and all her inhabitants and its weather—a sort of caretaking for future generations.

DRYAD

The forests are full of spirits and the Dryad is one. The Celtic Dryads are rumored to have taught their magic to the Druids. Also, a type of Greek Nymph, Dryads inhabit trees, living as the essence of the tree, for as long as the tree is alive. Dryads tend to be shy but will fiercely protect their tree habitat, if need be. They are particularly associated with the mighty oak tree—"drys" in Greek means "oak"—but do inhabit all types of trees. Their power and mystery lend the air of awe to the natural beauty of the forest we experience when among its gentle giants, the trees. Place your hand upon a tree's bark, close your eyes, and listen for its message.

DWARF

....

The Dwarf fairy likes to call Germany, the Swiss mountains, and parts of Scandinavia home. Typically small in stature, no bigger than a two-year-old, Dwarves can be quite beautiful or, more often, appear as old, bearded men, slightly stooped on occasion. They share many common physical characteristics of Gnomes (see page 53), and live in a similar habitat, using their superhuman strength digging tunnels throughout the mountains and working in the mines tending Earth's treasures, sometimes making exquisite jewelry with what they find. And, as great metal workers, Dwarves are renowned for using their powers to forge magical accoutrement, such as swords and rings. Dwarves can be solitary or trooping, and they can be kindly toward humans, or not, as they can be a capricious lot, occasionally donning their "cloak of invisibility" and disappearing altogether!

Dwarves can also take on the role of household spirit or helper, like the Brownie (see page 67) and Tomte (see page 70), excelling in their industriousness, responsibility, and general guardianship of homes in which they take up residence. And, despite their often brusque manner, Dwarves are quite sensitive beings, taking offense at even the slightest miscue, including being offered a fair wage for their work (they prefer food in appreciation, not money), and will leave without notice!

And despite their Germanic heritage, Dwarves populate other cultures, including various Native American tales.

Befriending a Dwarf can give you an ally, as they are said to be extremely wise, with their talents extending into seeing into the future, and they're generous as well, offering gold and jewels in payment for help provided to them. Their magic may come at a cost, though—and never be tempted to steal from or cheat the Dwarves: You will rue the day.

ELF

Hailing from Norse and Germanic folklore, these tiny, shape-shifting, pointy-eared fairies dwell in caves, forests, under rocks, and beneath springs. They are able to repel dark powers—yet are known to possess some as well. Today's Elves have grown into a more sophisticated persona, leaving behind the history of causing illness and seducing and abducting humans for one of a more industrious social character. Their magical abilities are said to stem from their ability to absorb and direct the energies around them—one reason for their deep concern for a healthy planet. They have extraordinary senses of sight and hearing, far beyond any human ability. The jolly Elves are known for their agility and grace and their ability to control the seas . . . from freezing to boiling and everything in between—especially when their dwellings are damaged. Weather is also at their command, for they can conjure storms or calm the winds on cue. Seeing into the future allows them to influence your fate. Where the four-leafed clover grows, Elves are said to tread.

FLOWER FAIRIES

These miniature, most charming of the Nature fairies correspond precisely with the flower each is tasked to tend and are everywhere a flower grows. They're dressed to match their namesake bloom and it's difficult to distinguish the flower from the fairy itself. Delightfully innocent, they flit, play, work, and dance among the flowers, fine-tuning scents and colors, arranging blossoms, and taste testing fruit by day, and sleep curled safely within the petals at night.

Each new flower seedling or tree blossom is a fairy about to be born. Each and every raindrop holds a Flower Fairy giggle waiting to be released. Every flower blossom is a fairy smile. The Flower Fairies earn, and demand, our respect of Mother Nature, and although a kindly spirit, they do not take kindly to those who defile Earth.

Each flower also has its own special message through the language of flowers, and so the fairies, as well, teach us through them. Each Flower Fairy inhabits the spirit of the flower, so the lavender fairy is calming, and the apple blossom fairy radiates loving beauty and clairvoyance. These joyous beings will tend to your garden and your spirit, with simple needs such as fresh water and sunshine—and a spot of privacy—in return for your tending to Nature.

GNOME

Though sometimes debated as to whether they are fairies, the Gnomes, also called Dwarves and Goblins, are of the element of earth and, as such, live underground roaming freely about in guardianship of Earth's hidden treasures, especially in the mines and quarries. They are typically small of stature and resemble a slightly stooped old man, with a sweet, bearded face and wear a jolly red cap. A Gnome's presence brings good luck and reassurance that their watchful attendance is on guard.

The Gnomes' workings of the earth aerate the soil and nourish the trees, which they endow with their powers of fertility. They are particularly fond of the oak tree and will sometimes reside there, closer to their animal friends, and Nature itself. Destruction of trees, especially the oak, can mean a very unhappy Gnome, which can mean a very unhappy human.

As demonstrated by their care of Earth, Gnomes are healing creatures and their energies can boost fertility and prosperity spells. They protect animals and humans with equal care. They are also particularly skilled at metalwork. A lovely necklace worn in their honor would be much appreciated. Display one in your garden, following long-standing tradition, to ensure a lush crop and a few laughs along the way.

LADY OF THE LAKE

Of mysterious origins, the Lady of the Lake's true identity is of debate—she may actually be several water fairies. The notable fairy queen beauty of Arthurian legend, who bestowed King Arthur with the magical sword, Excalibur, and to whom it was returned upon his death (as a sign to transport him to Avalon, where he would be tended) is one widely believed possibility. She also famously kidnapped Lancelot—some accounts credit her as being his godmother or stepmother—and reared him in her watery world, only to cure him of madness and instill in him the lessons that would guide him.

Viviane, or Nimue or Nineve, the enchanter who bewitched Merlin, then trapped him in a cave to keep as her own—not for love but for his magical knowledge—is another. Others suggest the Lady of the Lake descends from the Celtic water goddesses, including Brigid and Cerridwen, but specifically Coventina, as the name Viviane is a variation of that name.

She possesses the powers of other water elementals and was worshipped for her symbolism as giver of life. Offerings in her honor were frequently tossed in the waters surrounding her castle near Avalon and certainly included coins and other metal objects—and, perhaps, even Excalibur (no one knows for sure!). In addition, she is blessed with eternal beauty and the powers to create magical objects.

So, toss a coin in the nearest fountain in honor of the Lady of the Lake and thank her for her magical influence.

MENEHUNE

Hawaiian legend introduces us to the Menehunes, a slightly
mischievous—yet highly skilled and industrious—Dwarf race
who inhabits the mountain forests of these tropical islands from
the beginning of time. (It was noted by the first Hawaiian settlers
that there were roads, and ponds, and dams in existence all over
the islands when they arrived!) The Menehunes are a shy people,
preferring to stay out of sight, deep within the forests, but will come
out at night to work—when they feel like it—but only at night. In
the space of a single night, they could accomplish great feats of
engineering, such as building a road, or the great Menehune Ditch
that brought water to the townspeople, or a fish pond—their artistry
and execution so fine, many examples live on today. Though seen
by few, it is said that one hand given in friendship to a Menehune is
rewarded with the industrious work of their many hands. Dismiss
them at your own risk.

The Menehunes are not all work and no play: They make merry
by dancing and singing and enjoy diving contests, swimming, and
riding the dolphins and seagulls. They eat bananas and fish with
abandon. The Menehunes, a happy, peace-loving race, will not abide
anger—it's said, if you were angry, the Menehune would pierce
your unhappy heart with their magic arrows, which left love and
forgiveness to grow in its place.

MERFOLK

The familiar human-from-the-waist-up, fishtail-and-fins-below fairies live in deep oceans and seas. Tales of these sea creatures travel as far back as ancient Babylonian culture and, since then, have captured the imaginations of writers, poets, artists, musicians, and more, of all geographic regions and cultures—not to mention those who travel the seas for a living. They are variously described as having tails with scales, dolphinlike tails, forked tails, or just as mammals resembling a combination of fish and human.

The Mermaid is viewed as a manifestation of the fluidity and fertility of the water she inhabits, as well as its destructive nature. Musically talented, Mermaids, historically, do get a bad rap for luring sailors to their death with their hauntingly beautiful voices, but many are protective and bring good luck and wishes come true.

Like the Mermaid, the Siren of Greek mythology lives amidst the sea on its small rocky formations, but appears as a figure in the form of half bird and half beautiful young woman. Unlike the Mermaid, the Siren's motives are entirely untoward. With a voice as sweet as heavenly angels, the Siren lures unsuspecting sailors to her, only to destroy them once they approach too close.

In addition to the Selkie (see page 60), some other Mermaid accounts include the Mami Wata, meaning "Mother of the Waters," the water spirit in African culture, who is sometimes described as either a Mermaid or Merman and, sometimes, as a snake charmer. She is worshipped for her benevolent healing abilities as well as her charms to block evil.

Brazilian lore tells of the beautiful, green-eyed Iara, who lures sailors to her underwater palace; New Zealand's Māori people speak of Marakihau, with its human head, body of a very long fish, and lizard-like tongue that can leave destruction in its wake.

Russian folklore conjures the Rusalka, a mainly benevolent Mermaidlike creature who is credited with bringing water to crops in spring, but who came to be viewed as the ghost of women who drowned, and retaliated by luring unsuspecting victims and trapping them in her long hair.

And, in France, there is the sea spirit Melusine, a willful young girl who is thought to be the source of the French royal house of Lusignan.

Japan brings us tales of Ningyo, the monstrous looking human-headed fish that bestows eternal youth and beauty once eaten (if you dare!).

Carved mermaids were often used as figureheads on seafaring vessels as a way to appease the seas and ensure a safe journey.

NYMPH

Of Greek origin and said to be companions of the gods, Nymphs are female Nature spirits, distinct from Nature fairies by their more humanlike size, but similar in their natural habitat and guardianship of it. Nymphs can be found in forests, fields, mountains, rivers, oceans, and seas—really any natural place of beauty and wonder, anywhere in the world. Nymphs not only tend these great gifts, but created them as well. Encountering Nymphs is as easy as experiencing the awe that Nature inspires. With a generally kindly disposition and generous spirit, they occasionally frighten the solitary traveler when making themselves known, and can become angry when their home in Nature is defiled or disrespected. Act accordingly—the joyous energy you receive in return is your reward.

As there are so many wondrous natural resources, there are also numerous types of Nymphs. A few you may be particularly likely to meet along the way are:

- **Anthousai**, or flower Nymphs
- **Asteriai**, Nymphs who dance among the stars
- **Aurai**, swirl all around us as refreshing breezes
- **Dryads**, Tree Spirits (see page 63)
- **Epimelides** dwell among the pastures where they nurture the livestock and among the orchards that bear abundant sweet fruit

- **Hesperides**, the magnificent sunset Nymphs

- **Melissai**, Nymphs of the honeybee

- **Naiads**, freshwater spirits found among rivers, streams, wells, springs, and fountains

- **Nephelai**, rulers of the rain clouds

- **Nereids**, Nymphs of the deep sea

- **Oreiades**, mountain dwellers

SALAMANDER

The European fire spirit, the Salamander is akin to the Russian Firebird, Hindu Garuda, and even the English Hob. The Salamander's element is fire, which it breathes, controls, and dances in delight of. They are said to both be able to create fire as well as extinguish it. This fiery creature is passionate and a bit unpredictable, but works diligently to spread the light and keep the peace. When your internal flame is about to extinguish, seek a Salamander's spark to get you going again. Use the element of fire, responsibly, when you need to draw Salamander's energy, creativity, strength, and warmth to you.

SELKIE

Gentle, shape-shifting, sea-dwelling fairies from Scotland, Ireland, and Scandinavia, the Selkies, or seal people and relatives of the Merfolk, are frequently observed by humans bobbing in the sea waters watching and observing. Once a year, usually Midsummer's Eve, upon reaching shore, they shed their sealskins to transform into stunningly beautiful humans with enormously seductive powers. Here, they may live, love, dance, marry, bear children, and be happy but, ultimately, are destined to return to the sea, donning their sealskins again. The Selkie may be related to the Finfolk of Scandinavia, though these Finfolk are a more malevolent and mysterious family, with their rule over the seas and storms. And some think Selkies are humans living in the seas and oceans as Merfolk; others believe they're descended from the Japanese Swan Maidens.

SPRITE

A Sprite, whose name derives from the Latin word for spirit (*spiritus*) is a beautiful, magical fairy being, some say an older fairy, and maybe with a little less power, who dwells among Nature and all her creations and creatures. Known for their quickness and nimbleness, Sprites are easy creatures, usually working for good, but can also be up to no good on occasion. Sprites are often depicted as tiny, winged creatures who have an ethereal quality about them— leaving trails of sparkling fairy dust wherever they go.

Sprites can also be elementals, such as the water fairy, or water sprite, land sprite, and air sprite. *Water sprites* are known for their ability to breathe underwater, which they can transfer to you, and as guardians of the seas and sailors. *Air sprites* rule the air . . . conjuring breezes, storms, and rains and can carry you away on the wind. They also sing beautifully or can haunt with their whistles and howls. *Land sprites* love to dig in the dirt and grow things—they're a definite plus in your gardens to fertilize, weed, nourish, and harvest.

Sprites, in general, are fairly easy to keep happy just by offering a respectful nod, or gift, in their direction. Beware, though, the land sprite who burrows underground. Its tremors can be felt everywhere and will keep you unsettled and make your land unproductive.

SYLPH

These elemental pure-as-a-breath-of-fresh-air spirits live among the sky and the clouds, flying freely about, spreading joy and good will, and are among the weather forecasters and influencers of the fairy kingdom, as well as defenders of the environment. Though generally gentle magical beings, their temperaments can change like the wind. Described as a being not entirely spirit and not entirely physical, Sylphs are often depicted as graceful, winged fairies. They "clear the air," so to speak, and can help reset negative energies surrounding you.

Sylphs, also called Sylphids, are blessed with an uncanny clairvoyance. Though said to be the keepers of secrets—likely related to their complete understanding of the Universe and its intricate workings, the Sylphs are eager to share their knowledge with you, to help buffer the winds of change, and keep you on the right path. Though so innocent they are unable to be seen by humans, when a Sylph is nearby, you may feel a breeze or sudden wind gust, and you'll feel an incredible lightness and joy, and may spontaneously burst into song and dance.

Sylphs are not naturally immortal, though, and may die from hunger or injury. Protect and nourish any Sylph who befriends you to prolong their life—but be forewarned there may be more to the friendship: Sylphs are said to gain immortality once married to a human!

TREE SPIRITS

Many cultures seek the wisdom and favor of their Tree Spirits. They are symbols of fertility and health; they provide shelter for wildlife and humans and their bounty nourishes. Tree Spirits can take the form of fairies, Sprites, Nymphs, ghosts, and even goddesses.

The Flower Fairies (see page XX) also tend to and reside within the flowering trees, contributing to each tree's unique personality, but there are also fairies and spirits whose main job is to protect (some say haunt!) the forest and its trees. Consider:

The *Canotila*, forest spirits from Native American Sioux folklore, manifest as Sprites or Dwarves living within the forest's trees and are respected and anticipated as messengers of the spirit realm. They are wise teachers of the powers and spirit of the forests and living in harmony with them.

The *Dryads* (see page 49) of Greek myth are beautiful Nymphs who live among the forests and the trees, especially among the oaks, which were thought to hold the wisdom of the future. Hamadryads specifically inhabit a particular tree, becoming its soul and spirit, and living only as long as the tree itself. They are responsible for caring for their tree for life.

Gillie Dhu lives deep within the forests of Scotland, guarding them from intruders, specifically adult intruders. He favors the birch tree and stays out of sight, camouflaging himself with leaves, twigs, and branches, emerging from his home only at night. Gillie Dhu is particularly fond of children, though, who play amongst the forest realm, and he will watch over them and protect them when they are within its arms.

Huldra, tempter of the forest, is often compared to the Mermaid of the sea. Bewitchingly lovely, her beauty is irresistible to those who see her, despite knowing of its associated risks. Her most defining feature—a cow's tail—is a sure giveaway that Huldra is, indeed, your beckoning suitor.

Kodama, an ancient Japanese Tree Spirit, is variously thought to inhabit the trees of the forest, or just specific trees, or to be the spirit of the tree indistinguishable from the tree itself, or a tree-dwelling Goblin. In all its forms, Kodama is revered for its gifts of fruits, seeds, lumber, shelter, wisdom, and more. These powerful spirits could be your ally and protector when respected, or your worst nightmare when damaged or disrespected.

Leshy guards the Russian forest and rules above all who live there. Depicted with wild hair about his head and face, he is a shape-shifter and mischievous trickster. Keep close to the forest path to avoid his attempts to mislead. When leaves drop from the trees in fall, this signals Leshy's annual winter slumber. He awakens in spring with a shaking of his limbs as buds burst into bloom. Should you seek the forest for its supplies, always leave an offering for Leshy in gratitude.

The *Moss People*, who appear, well, dressed in moss, hail from Germany and Central Europe and are a tree's guardian spirit. A wise, elderly spirit, the Moss People generously share their knowledge of forest flora and its healing abilities, unless it is disrespected . . . at which time you'll be chased off the premises.

UNDINE

The bewitchingly beautiful Undine is an invisible spirit of the element water, inhabiting, manipulating, and protecting all the watery regions of our planet, where the flow of emotion is ruled by the Moon. Undines hail from the ancient Greek Nereids, consorts of the sea god Poseidon. The Mermaid belongs to the Undine family.

The Undine is an eager helper to sailors and is known to be a faithful companion to all who travel the seas. An Undine may lure unsuspecting water travelers with its haunting songs borne on the wind, but will not do them harm, like their cousins, the Sirens. Sometimes, Undines seek a human mate in order to become human. Respond with purity of intentions, as any Undine betrayed will die.

The Undine's size depends on habitat, with ocean-living fairies being larger than those found in small ponds or even fountains. Undines are drawn to mortals with a water sign and will respond to communication helped by "watery" crystals, such as amethyst, aquamarine, amazonite, and opal.

Keep fresh water on hand for any Undine to refresh itself and be open to their go-with-the-flow attitude. A sudden sun shower—or a good cry—and the fresh cleansing it brings, the sparkle of the dew, the mist of a fog, or the prism of color in a sunlit raindrop are sure signs an Undine is with you.

HOUSEHOLD AND HELPER FAIRIES

Originally thought to be linked to the land where a house was built, in which they would then take up residence, house fairies, or house spirits, are generally benevolent shape-shifting creatures who often manifest as the animals in the home. They have many names, depending on their country or region of origin, and are simple spirits, expecting nothing in return for their work except a little sustenance, preferring milk, honey, and bread to keep them happy. If you have house fairies dwelling among your family, they're often sensed or heard before being seen, as they're usually only visible to those with the sight, or who truly believe. House fairies often attach to one member of the household and don't abide noise or mess. They're eager to please—but can be mischievous if they're not happy about some slight they may perceive. In addition to their industriousness around the home helping with chores and tending to the animals and land, house fairies can heal, bless, delight, and conjure abundance.

BROWNIE

....

Long recounted in English and Scottish tales, the Brownie, or Hob
(known as the Kobold in German lore), is a solitary little home fairy.
This seldom-seen but oft-heard Gnomelike spirit loves the rural
dwelling or farm where he can help the homeowner by sweeping
and cleaning and tending to chores to his heart's content . . . usually
at night under cover of darkness. If it's dirt your home needs
protecting from or animals that need feeding, leave out some sweet
milk or cream, or even cake, to entice this fine fellow in. Although
industrious and clearly talented, the Brownie can be temperamental.
He can make others, especially lazy servants, look bad just for his
own good, and he accepts no payment or reward for his work, which
is said to drive him away. Beware his cousin, the Hobgoblin, though,
who is only out for mischief—at your home's expense! If this fate
befalls you, make the gift of fine clothes to, it's said, set him free.

CHIN CHIN KOBAKAMA

....

This Japanese house fairy is a stickler for cleanliness, especially
regarding the home's traditional woven straw tatami mats, which
historically are trod upon only when wearing socks or with bare
feet to keep them as clean as possible. If a home is clean, the Chin
Chin Kobakama will bless the home with great good luck. If it's not
clean, this Elflike fairy will torment the home's lazy inhabitants to no
end. Small children are often teased mercilessly when they dirty the
mats in the home. Lazy housekeepers will meet the same fate if they
are not careful and considerate of the home's clean atmosphere.
Though tiny and wizened, these fairies are unendingly energetic.
Keep a broom handy if you want to stay in their good graces. They'll
even pitch in if they feel you're doing your share of the housework.

DOMOVOI

Head of the house he is . . . oh, you thought that was you? Well, he'll let you think that. Descending from Slavic tradition, this otherworldly house sprite, like the Brownie, attaches to a family and, when in a good mood, will faithfully serve and protect. Keep him happy, though, or mischief ensues. He is particularly fond of children and pets. The Domovoi takes his mission seriously to protect the home from spiritual and physical harm.

Those who have seen him say he is a hairy, scary, frightening little figure . . . but those people are not many. The Domovoi prefers to stay out of sight. His presence is felt long before he is seen. Misplaced your keys? Hearing footsteps at night? Animals are active? (Probably work of the Domovoi!)

The Domovoi is happiest when all in the home is in order; he dislikes a mess and is offended by harsh language. He appreciates a moment of silent acknowledgment when you will be away from home. A light supper of milk and bread, or leftovers, is appreciated, too, to keep him happy and motivated.

MAZZAMURELLO, AND HIS COUSIN, MONACIELLO

The whimsical Italian Elf, Mazzamurello, is Italy's incarnation of the Irish Leprechaun. He is known for his kindness and generosity to good people and for his tricks and scare tactics to those who are bad, but has an annoying habit of making things disappear around the house (which he will return when he feels like it, or when you've given up any hope of finding them!). His presence will become unquestionably known by the continuous banging sounds he makes on walls (sometimes even demolishing them in the process). If you dare follow him, Mazzamurello will lead you to treasure (or not, depending on his mood). He is also said to bring messages from deceased loved ones.

Mazzamurello's cousin, Monaciello, "Little Monk," lives exclusively in Naples, Italy, and is so tiny he can gain entrance to your home through a keyhole. Like his cousin, he is noisy and likes to hide things, but prefers to come out at night, stealing the covers from unsuspecting sleepers. He, too, can lead you to his hidden treasure; an easier way to get it may just be to steal his red hat, for which he will pay a ransom of gold coins to have it back. Monaciello adores any children in the home and rewards them with sweets and coins, and will go out of his way to help with chores, so the children don't have to do them.

TOMTE

Solitary and slightly mischievous, the Tomte takes up residence on Scandinavian farms, guarding and tending the land, animals, family, barn, and homestead. This short, old, white-bearded, red-capped little man is also known as Nisse in Norway. Legend tells us that Tomte originates from the spirit of the original farm owner, who returns to ensure the health and continuity of the farm.

Tomte is a fierce protector, his work ethic is impeccable, and he is loyal and industrious—unless interfered with, when obnoxious behavior ensues. He is not a team player. Tomte's help and contribution to running the household are much-valued commodities to farm owners—even their companionship (though they do like to keep out of sight, being most active at night) can ease the long, hard winters of living off the land. Keeping him happy is easy: respect, order, cleanliness, peace, and butter are simple keys to living in harmony with Tomte. Rudeness, disrespect, mistreating animals, ignoring him, and a stressful environment are likely causes for him to abandon your home.

The little one is especially fond of Christmas and goes into a frenzy cooking, cleaning, decorating, baking, and taking care of all the little details that make the time so special for everyone. A sweet bowl of Christmas porridge topped with a generous pat of butter is all he asks in return.

TRASGU

Spanish lore gives us their equivalent of the Irish Leprechaun, a lovably mischievous red hat-wearing Sprite who, once tamed, becomes a loyal household helper. Don't expect complete domesticity, though; a bit of unruliness is part of life. He is difficult to be rid of, so treat Trasgu well and enjoy the benefits of the nightly chores he tackles.

ZASHIKI WARASHI

These adorable house spirits hail from Japan and are vigilant guardians of the home, said to be bearers of good luck. Though seldom seen—usually only by a home's owner or children in the home—and appearing as young children, they are often heard instead. They love a good prank—your first indication that Zashiki Warashi have settled in may be a child's powdery footprints all over the home.

Zashiki Warashi usually take up residence in a guest room and love to amuse children. Elderly and childless couples love them as their own. Their presence in a house foretells of fortune and success, and their home guardianship is so valued that they are eagerly courted. Offerings of food and drink, as well as coins built into a new home's foundation, are said to be attractive to the Zashiki Warashi. If one befriends your home, count your blessings.

OTHER FAIRIES: ANGELIC FAIRIES, PRANKSTERS, AND TROUBLE

This fairy group may seem diverse but as fairies, those beings believed to have originated as fallen angels, they definitely share common origins. As individual fairies they diverge based on their path chosen: Some fallen angels continue in their angelic ways, to bring love and light and hope and healing to humans and Earth. Others get bored easily and love a good trick or two at our expense. Still others have passed into the evil realm of seduction, abduction, and wreaking havoc where they tread. Let's look a bit more closely, if you dare.

BALLYBOG

Known by various names, the Ballybog is also called Peat Fairy, Boggle, Bog-a-Boo, and Boggie, to name a few. Found in England, Wales, and Ireland, the Ballybog is charged with protecting the peat bogs, most of which can be found in Ireland where peat is a source of fuel. This round, froglike, croaking, mud-covered fairy thrives in a damp, dark, marshy environment and is a loner by nature. The preserved human remains found throughout Ireland's peat bogs spurred ancient tales of human sacrifices made to the bog fairies to keep them happy and afford protection to the one leaving the offering. It's often told, too, of the bog choosing its own victim and slowly swallowing them whole in the spongy peat—just like quicksand. Although the Ballybog is usually too busy to cause any real trouble, if you find yourself a solitary traveler through the marshes and bogs, beware: You may suddenly find yourself lost among the mist to the amusement of the fairies.

BEAN-SIDHE, OR BANSHEE

This Celtic fairy is known for her mournful cries and harrowing shrieks—said to shatter glass—that predict death and doom. Those who have seen her call her beautiful, or disheveled, old, and withered. Her fiery-red eyes weep constantly for loss. She will attach herself to a specific family and be watchful of the children throughout their lives. Though often appearing to foretell a physical death, Bean-sidhe can also portend any type of ending, such as of a relationship, or signal the need to let go of something no longer serving us. Her appearance is feared, yet she is not an evil spirit.

Similar spirits, the Celtic Bean-nighe, a fairy washerwoman, is thought to be the ghost of a woman who has died in childbirth and who inhabits streams or ponds washing the blood-stained clothes of the dead, and La Llorona in Latin American tradition, haunts streams and rivers, mourning her drowned children.

Give these spirits room to mourn, but do not be afraid.

CLURICHAUN

Cousin to the industrious Leprechaun, the Clurichaun is more likely to drink all your beer and wine than tend to that hole in your shoe. Often mistaken for each other, there are key differences between these two fairies. The Clurichaun tends to be clean-shaven and prefers flashier clothes than the earth tones favored by Leprechauns. The Clurichaun appears and disappears at will, and loves nothing better than a good story—except that drop of whisky to go with it. If you find yourself in the company of the Clurichaun, keep him fed (to avoid hangovers) and happy (to avoid ill fortune). Left alone to guard your wine cellar, he's steadfast in his duties, and may even leave you a dram or two, if you ask nicely.

CHANGELING LORE

Fairies are feared for bringing changelings into people's lives—stealing healthy human newborns and leaving in exchange a sick fairy child in its place. The human infant could be given to the devil in sacrifice or integrated in the Fairy Realm.

FAIRY GODMOTHER

Some argue the Fairy Godmother has existed in the fairy kingdom since the times of King Arthur, and others say she is a more modern invention created in the retelling of certain fairy tales, such as *Cinderella* and *Sleeping Beauty*. Fairy lore depicts her as a mysterious spiritual being who suddenly appears at births or christenings to bless (or curse!) a child and bestow special abilities on the babe. A Fairy Godmother is the granter of wishes and protector from harm and, like human godmothers, her role is to look after the spiritual health of the child. She may stay with you briefly or reappear throughout your life, offering wisdom and guidance. Whatever you believe, if you have one, thank your lucky stars.

GOBLIN

....

The Goblin is not your friend. This mountain-dwelling fairy is, at once, ugly, greedy, mean, and troublesome. Goblins dwell deep within Earth protecting her mines and treasures and are apt to get in the way of anyone who goes exploring there. They love wreaking havoc and playing tricks, but will also steal your possessions the first chance they get—Goblins are especially fond of stealing horses. Goblins are known to possess magical powers, but don't often use them for good. Weaving nightmares is a typical pastime.

A cousin, the Hobgoblin, is more industrious and known to be a helper around the house, though moody and temperamental about it, and is prone to slightly less evil ways of entertaining himself at others' expense!

LEPRECHAUN

....

This lively fellow prefers sartorial choices of green from head to toe, but will wear red occasionally. The Leprechaun is a solitary fairy who practices shoemaking as a profession, and it is noted he is highly skilled at it. He is a bit of a hoarder by nature (How do you think he got that pot of gold?) and somewhat mischievous to boot.

That storied pot of gold is kept at the end of the rainbow. If you're lucky enough to find—and catch—a Leprechaun, you'll be granted three wishes in exchange for his freedom (that is if you're not hit with a blinding burst of fairy dust first to hide his escape!). Listen for the tap!-tap!-tap! of his hammer to know he is nearby.

PERI

Another trickster, the Peris are beautiful, winged fairies whose origins are in ancient Persia. Much like other trickster fairies, Peris are neither good nor evil, but do enjoy keeping humans on their toes . . . hiding car keys, misplacing glasses, moving objects from their usual places, and the like. Don't overlook Peris' presence, as this fairy usually brings messages from other spirit realms.

PIXIE

Pixies are kind, tiny, childlike creatures with merry souls whose mirth bubbles over for all to enjoy. Hailing from southwest England, these tiny beings often sport gossamer wings. With pretty faces and cute pointed noses and ears, they look innocent and trustworthy, but be on guard—Pixies love a prank. They flourish among the flowers— where the flowers flourish as well—and are helpful with chores. Their true home, though, is among the bogs and forests of the southern English countryside where they can be found dancing to the nocturnal sounds under a Full Moon or stealing a horse or two for a wild midnight ride. A Pixie's magic is enchanting—to fall under its spell is to dance among the fairies. As a traveler, beware the Pixie encounter as they find great amusement in leading one astray—if Pixie-led you be, wandering about aimlessly, take solace in knowing it's temporary.

ROBIN GOODFELLOW, A.K.A. PUCK

Don't be fooled by "goodfellow" in his name—that comes from the habit of humans complimenting "the Good People" to keep them happy. This shape-shifting impish, some say devilish, fairy is friends with, perchance related to, the Hobgoblin, and is the personification of the trickster we also know as Puck. A talented, controlling, and hardworking fellow, Robin puts himself in charge of household chores to keep a tidy ship—to the same exacting standards applied in Fairyland—but he delights in tormenting and teasing servants, family, and guests at the same time.

Simultaneously, his racket is a bit like the bully in the lunchroom who won't steal your lunch for a price . . . which he often did not reveal until after helping the overworked head of household with the daily chores. To keep the peace, at the very least, a bucket of clean water in which to bathe and a dish of milk and hunk of bread each night can go a long way to satisfy Robin. The Irish Pooka is a similar household spirit. Be on guard against their devilish charm—the price may just be too high to pay.

SEELIE COURT

The Seelie Court division of fairies in the Celtic-Scottish traditions is the peaceable kingdom of magical fairies who were kindly and good and of help to their human counterparts (especially those in need or anyone who showed them kindness), save for the occasional prank, or ill nature when their privacy is invaded, or their territory disrespected.

The Seelie Court is considered the aristocratic tier of fairy society. They enjoy music, singing, dancing, hunting (for the chase, though, not the kill), chess, ball games, and processionals, like their traditional fairy rades. The famous "Londonderry Air" is a favorite song of these fairies, even rumored to have been composed by a band of fairies playing a harp found by the river's side. (The tune was originally known as "O'Cahan's Lament," as it was his harp the fairies were playing, because he dropped it in a drunken stupor on the way home from the pub!) Extremely accomplished human musicians were sometimes abducted to Fairyland for their musical talents alone. Keep watch if that describes you!

Seemingly constantly at war with the Unseelie Court, these good fairies are just trying to keep order among their own.

TOOTH FAIRY

Most of us today already have a firmly established relationship with one fairy—the Tooth Fairy. She (the Tooth Fairy is generally a kindly, motherly figure), however, is a fairly new age fairy as fairies go, making herself known at about the start of the nineteenth century, and celebrates the magic that is growing up. The Tooth Fairy appears to be especially American in origin, though the custom of "disposing" of children's shed teeth as they grow is distinctly global in scope and includes such customs as burying them, throwing them into the fire, or offering the lost tooth as a sacrifice . . . to a mouse!— in hopes the child's adult teeth will turn out as strong. Even today, the "Tooth Mouse" will swap teeth for gifts, including cash.

Helping ease the fear of shedding body parts (!), the Tooth Fairy lends an air of celebration to the event of losing one's baby teeth. All a believing child needs to do is place that shiny tooth under their pillow at bedtime and the Tooth Fairy will find it—and leave a monetary reward in exchange for it. The national average is close to $4 these days!

The Tooth Fairy is both talented and clever and finds multiple uses for the many hundreds of thousands of teeth she collects. She builds and repairs her tooth castle, collects the best of the lot for display, grinds them for fairy dust, makes jewelry, gives them as gifts to newborns and the elderly who have lost their natural teeth, fashions amulets for good luck and protection, and tosses them to the sky where new stars are born.

As elusive as any magical fairy, she just may reveal herself to children more easily than adults! I bet you've seen her more than once—after all, she's visited you about twenty times over the course of those baby teeth falling out—but the wisdom of age says you couldn't have possibly seen her. Never stop believing!

UNSEELIE COURT

In Celtic-Scottish traditions, the Unseelie Court—the wicked wight, or creature—comprises a variety of wretched, ill-tempered fairies who are a bad lot, with a deservedly bad reputation. Generally solitary in nature, living a hardscrabble existence in the deep wilderness, these fairies came into being, having given themselves over to the devil in some way and they thrive on distress and danger. These malevolent characters are unfeeling and unable to be charmed or befriended. They are associated with another fairy court, the Winter Court, personifying its cold, cruel, dark, inhospitable nature. Avoid them at all costs.

WILL-O'-THE-WISP

An elemental fiery fairy, Will-o'-the-Wisp is well-known in England, but also in Ireland, Scotland, Wales, Denmark, Netherlands, Germany, the United States, Asian countries such as China, India, Japan, and Thailand, South American countries such as Brazil and Peru, and other countries of the world. This fairy goes by a number of aliases, including Jack-o'-Lantern, Kitty Candlestick, Herrwisch, and Friar's Lantern.

This fiery fairy is typically spied at night, appearing as a ghostly glow, reflection, or flickering flame hovering above the ground—"wisp" is the bits of hay or bundles of sticks they use as their torch to light the way. The lights can look benign, or perhaps, like a signal for help. They haunt marshy bogs and waylay unsuspecting passersby. Their trickster nature makes itself known from Will-o'-the the-Wisp's habit of leading travelers astray with their lantern lights—sometimes into deadly danger; sometimes into the fairy kingdom (and never to be heard from again!); and sometimes to spots of buried treasure. Whether as trickster or helper, Will-o'-the-Wisp often leads one to their fate. As such, this fairy is deemed either an omen of death or an illuminator of the path to reward. Should you spot one of these creatures, it is up to you to decide if the risk is worth the potential reward of following Will-o'-the-Wisp.

Communicating with the Fairies

Fairies surround our lives with their magical presence. If you're highly intuitive, you may sense them with ease. Intuition can be developed, so worry not if yours needs a little help.

Key to communicating with fairies is communing with Nature, where their energy is at its highest. Enticing the fairies into your world and learning to work with them is as simple as opening your heart and holding your true beliefs and desires there. Learn their names, invite them to journal or meditate with you, discover their favorite crystals or other natural elements to work with. Do something nice for them! Just as when making new friends, showing interest in them will draw them to you. Following are some simple, and more complex ways to increase your fae folk acquaintance.

FAIRY COMMUNICATION ETIQUETTE

airies are discerning when it comes to human interaction. They're easily enticed and easily annoyed. Sometimes they just want to be left alone. Animals are almost guaranteed a fairy companion, but so are certain people: lovers, to be sure, are under the watchful eye of fairy guardians. To ensure you present your most welcoming self to these delightful spirits, keep the following tips in mind:

- Be openminded.
- Be willing and able to keep a secret—not all fairies want publicity.
- Be respectful of their privacy.
- Be generous.
- Be truthful.
- Be humble.
- Be polite.
- Be neat and orderly.
- Be hospitable.
- Be joyous.
- Sing and dance!

FIVE INTUITIVE SENSES

*Claircognizance * Clairsalience * Clairaudience * Clairsentience * Clairvoyance*

"Clair" Senses

Your "clair," or clear, intuitive senses are the psychic equivalent of your five senses, and in each of us, one or more may be more active than others.

Fairy energies exists all around us, combined with all other energies. Our "clair" senses are keys to helping us unlock their presence and messages for more meaningful work with the fae. Children and animals seem to demonstrate high degrees of skills in these areas, likely due to their innocent view of the world. Adults must learn to open their minds and hearts to the unexplainable, yet undeniable, joys of the Fairy Realm—joys only heightened by their connection with Nature.

- Do you have particularly strong premonitions that prove true or amazing instincts? That's *claircognizance*, or the knowing of something we have no way of proving we know.

- Perhaps you smell a deceased loved one's favorite flowers or foods at holidays, or cigarette smoke in the house, with no obvious source? That's *clairsalience*.

- *Clairaudience* equates to sounds received and heard that others may not hear—but the messages and ideas are clear to you.

- *Clairsentience* is a kind of psychic empathy that's felt physically, giving you that gut reaction to someone new or the goosebumps we develop in certain situations.

- A visual flash of something in your mind's eye, past or present, while awake or dreaming, sends us a message through *clairvoyance*. All psychic senses can be developed, and all require a bit of faith in how they work. Try Crystal Clear Intuition (page 156) to work on yours.

COMMUNICATING AND WORKING
WITH THE FAIRIES

Working with the fairies requires clear, honest communication, and they, in turn, communicate in all ways to humans . . . you may hear the buzzing of bees when fairies are nearby, or feel the brush of a breeze, or spot a sparkle of light. You may pick up messages in your head when they're not expected (that song that won't go away?!) or find evidence of their presence with sweet floral aromas or found objects nearby. Perhaps it's the coincidental sighting of a bird or other animal, the chill of a sudden mist, or just the feeling of joy that tingles through your body. Fairies can also make themselves known while journaling and meditating, during Moon magic practices (particularly during the Full Moon—a time they're said to relish and be most active), and, of course, when working with crystals, herbs, and flowers, or any other elements of Nature.

The fae's energy is of creativity, inspiration, magical intent, and manifestation. However you sense or invite them into your magical practice, fairies are magical beings that will serve to enhance your magical energies. Let's look more closely at ways to communicate with the fairies—and their magical energies—we want to entice into our life.

JOURNALING

When journaling—whether about specific issues and intentions, everyday thoughts and plans, or just tracking your fairy garden's growth, invite the fairies to work with you. A simple smile is a great place to start, then sit in quiet communication, asking for their thoughts and help in reaching your goals and removing obstacles in your way.

Let the fairies work through you as you journal—you may discover new thoughts and ideas in the process to motivate and guide your plans, and your creativity is bound to sparkle. This is also a place to record your fairy interactions, whether seen or felt. You may also discover the fae reveal themselves to you in new ways, expanding your access to their magical powers. Journaling is also a way to cultivate a habit of gratitude, which can serve you well in building your fairy community.

- Journal daily, or only as needed, but make space in your life to let the magic in.

- Record any spontaneous thoughts or feelings, as well as your specific intentions and plans to manifest them.

- Write about your inner fairy needs and desires.

- Decorate your journal with drawings or images, poetry or spells that evoke the fairy folk.

- Write down questions you wish to explore with the fairies or record times you felt their presence, including where you were and what you were doing. How did you know they were with you? Let your writing channel their message.

- Imagine yourself as a fairy and write about your special powers. Write freely and honestly—without judgment.

- Create affirmations that channel fairy energy.

- Journal about spells and rituals you've tried and created as well as their results.

Whatever you desire to manifest, putting your intentions into writing creates a record to serve as a reminder as well as one you can reflect on and check in on for progress along the way. Putting things in writing, in general, moves us from the "thought" stage to the "action" stage. It keeps you committed, motivated, focused, reminded. It frees up space in your brain for other things. It keeps you grateful and honest. It can reduce stress. Writing about your dreams and intentions creates another form of energy to release your thoughts into the Universe.

MEDITATING WITH THE FAIRIES

Another useful tool to connect with fairy energy and their magic is mindful meditation, which offers the chance to slow down and reflect, to invite the fairies to be with you and tap into their wisdom, while exploring your inner thoughts and feelings.

Mindful meditation is the practice of being present, *in the moment without judgment*, and paying attention to yourself—your breathing, emotions, sensations, and thoughts. Meditation is not about tuning out everything in our lives but, rather, tuning in to the present and being with ourselves.

Mindful meditation takes practice and consistency. Even ten minutes a day can help, but once you begin to feel the benefits in your life, you will crave the quiet peace that meditation affords.

Fairy Meditation Basics

- **Find a quiet, comfortable place** where you won't be disturbed. Relax. Set a gentle alarm if you wish to time your session.

- **Close your eyes**, if you are comfortable doing so, to limit visual distractions.

- **Ask**. Invite a specific fairy to join you, or let one select you. Visualize your fairy companion entering your space, sitting with you, walking with you, communicating with you, comforting you. What can you sense? How do you feel?

- **Breathe**. Bring your attention to your breathing. Breathe naturally, yet fully. Feel your body grow on the in-breath and feel it collapse on the out-breath. Feel your breath calming and centering you.

- **Imagine** each inhale fills you with fairy magic and love—from top to bottom—cleansing and clearing any negativity, hurt, or fear.

- **Visualize** your exhale taking with it anything causing you pain as you replace it on the inhale with soothing kindness and infinite magical power.

- **Focus**. Keep your attention on your breath. When your mind wanders, gently acknowledge it and return your focus to your breath. Listen to the magic within.

- **Be grateful**. When your timer sounds, or you are ready, return your focus to your surroundings. Open your eyes. Wiggle your toes. Take a moment to acknowledge the Wee Folk for the quiet time and be grateful for the space that welcomes you before returning to your normal activities—charged with an energy that both soothes and inspires.

PLANNING A FAIRY GARDEN

In the spirit of tending to Nature, a favorite way to connect with and entice the fairies into your life is to plan, plant, and tend a garden dedicated to them. Plus, welcoming fairies into your garden not only boosts the plants' innate magical properties but amplifies your magical work as well. To make certain the invitation to take up residence is well received, keep these tips in mind as you try to tempt the fairies in.

꩜ BE KIND: Fairies favor those who care for and nurture Earth and her waterways and keep its creatures happy . . . feed the birds; be kind to all wildlife. Keep up with your garden chores, like weeding and cleaning up plant decay, to keep things tidy and healthy.

꩜ BE INVITING: Invite fairies into your garden with kind thoughts and deeds. When you're out working among the plants, invite the fairies to work alongside you in harmony with Nature, or point out specific plants they may like . . . a lush carpet of elfin thyme for napping, bright marigolds to serve as lanterns, or beautiful bee balm as a source of refreshing tea. Create a fairy door in an old tree as a sign of welcome and to afford a little privacy.

BE GENEROUS: Fairies love flowers, lots and lots of flowers. Among those you choose to add to your garden, consider including some dear to the fairies (see page 96).

BE PROTECTIVE: Provide shelter . . . a fairy is at home in Nature, so include plants in your herb garden with large leaves or other features to provide shelter from sunshine and rain.

BE NURTURING: As for all of Nature, and especially water fairies, water is a must . . . a birdbath or butterfly pond will enchant and delight as a spot for bathing and drinking and if you're lucky enough to live near a body of water, such as a pond, river, lake, or stream, be vigilant in keeping it clean and inviting.

BE ENTERTAINING: Fairies love bling. If you can, place some crystals in your garden or a reflective gazing ball. Music helps, too. Wind chimes can tempt with their soothing charms. Bell-shaped flowers invite the fairies to play their own tunes. Establish a fairy ring as a signal for merriment.

BE GRATEFUL: Offerings, especially milk and honey, and gifts of fresh-cut herbs, are believed to be particularly welcoming to the fae.

PLANTING AND TENDING A FAIRY GARDEN—FLOWERS, HERBS, AND TREES

Any plants beloved by bees, butterflies, and hummingbirds (a garden's earthly fairies) will also appeal to potential fairy tenants. Each will add a unique element to your fairy paradise and will, in turn, each be guarded by its own fairy protector.

- **Bluebells** encourage laughter and merriment.

- **Butterfly bush** provides sweet nectar and butterfly friends.

- **Cabbage leaves** make a lovely fairy tub in which to bathe.

- **Chives** afford protection.

- **Columbine** for fun.

- **Day lily** provides a source of magic wands for the fairies.

- **Elder tree**, called "the tree of music" by some; its branches make lovely recorders, flutes, and whistles—a favorite of the music-making fairy kingdom. Listen for the fairy band dancing beneath the boughs. It is said that to sleep under the elder is to dance among the fairies.

- **Elecampane** is a favorite fairy tool of the Elves.

- **Ferns**, for shelter (and invisibility, see page 169).

- **Foxglove**, though poisonous, is a beloved fairy planting, providing shelter.

- **Fuchsia blossoms** make lovely fairy skirts and their sweet nectar delights.

- **Hawthorn tree**, the legendary tree of the fairies—a place so sacred, grave harm may befall any who deface it. Portals to magical realms are said to exist beneath the flowering hawthorn, whose white flowers signal a return of the fairies in late spring.

- **Hazel tree**, whose delightful nuts are a favorite among garden fairies.

- **Heather**, when slept upon, opens the door to the Fairy Realm.

- **Irish moss** lays a magical carpet.

- **Lavender** helps relax and renew.

- **Lily of the valley** are the flower wind chimes of the fairy garden.

- **Marigold** lights the fairy world, shining with sunny optimism.

- **Mugwort** is a magically potent Midsummer herb and a favorite of the Fairy Realm.

- **Nasturtium**, to spice things up.

- ❧ **Pansies** for their cheery little fairy faces and the joyful love they spread.

- ❧ **Roses** to entice all manner of fairies who will protect and nurture the plants.

- ❧ **Strawberries** provide sweet sustenance.

- ❧ **Thyme** is perfect for fairy crowns and said to bring good luck.

- ❧ **Violet** is a traditional fairy plant with a sweet scent that soothes, and its heart-shaped leaves offer a place to sit and contemplate.

- ❧ **Wild rose** is a particular fairy favorite said to bloom where there is love.

When You Spy Fairy Dust . . .

The truest signs of fairies residing in your garden are lush, thriving flowers and herbs and the tantalizing scents wafting on the wind; maybe even a glint off the water when the Sun's not shining. You might also feel a slight brush of a breeze across your cheek when working in the garden . . . from a kiss of a fairy's gossamer wings. You may even spy a fairy ring (do not disturb it!), where a dance or two has likely occurred—or create one from crystals or stones as a sign of welcome and take a moment to be grateful for the bounty around you as you listen for the sounds of music and laughter. If you listen well, you may even hear the flowers and leaves singing in harmony—and see the butterflies and ladybugs dancing, for they are a sure sign fairies are nearby. Be respectful of your new magical friends and they will tend to your magical garden with love.

MIDSUMMER EVE

Summer solstice is a time of heightened activity in the fairy kingdom. Take advantage of the super-charged magical environment, not only to be out among the fairies, but to gather the bounty from your midsummer fairy garden, as the herbs' magic will be at its most potent. Among the midsummer herbs to gather are elder blossoms (but no napping under the tree or you risk offending the fairies), ivy, lavender, lemon balm, mugwort, mullein, and vervain.

MAGICAL FAIRY TOOLS

Working your fairy magic does not require any special tools. In fact, the only necessary tool is *you* and the magical enchantment and belief you find in connecting with Universal energies to influence outcomes. That said, if you'd like to incorporate some tools into your fairy magic practice to amplify your intentions and the enchantment factor of your spells, take inspiration from the fairies themselves, or from tools you already are comfortable using in your daily magic, and consider adding some new things to try.

There is no secret to which tools are better than others—it's the tool that calls to you or makes you feel magical or produces the best results. Here, we'll explore some ideas to get your sparkling magic flowing and that just might attract a fairy friend. Feel free to experiment with any ideas you have.

CREATING A FAIRY ALTAR

A fairy altar can be a fun space to create and use in your magical practice to inspire your work and manifest the vibrational energy you'll use to release intentions into the Universe and invite the fairies to join you. An altar defines your sacred space and provides a visual reminder and a physical presence—inside or outside, when working in groups or alone—to focus your energy, meditate, or try a fairy spell or two.

Your altar does not have to be fancy and can be as simple as a windowsill or cardboard box. It can even be a shelf or tabletop where you display your fairy tarot cards, candles, crystals, or other reminders of your intentions and priorities, to keep you aware every day of the work you're doing.

You may even decide to have more than one altar—one inside and one outside to celebrate Nature's beauty and the fairies who live among it, changing with the seasons, honoring Nature and your life's intentions as they grow and evolve.

You can also create altars reflecting specific intentions: Set up an altar in your bedroom devoted to romance; one in the kitchen to conjure abundance; one in a quiet corner for cultivating gratitude or gathering strength; even one in the bathroom for cleansing and renewing rituals. Maybe you'll create one dedicated to your ancestors. Be as fancy, creative, or minimalist as you like (remember, fairies love shiny objects!).

Your altar represents you—your heart, hopes, dreams, intentions, and life. If you stay true to your heart, your altar will be ready to help you work your magic when called upon.

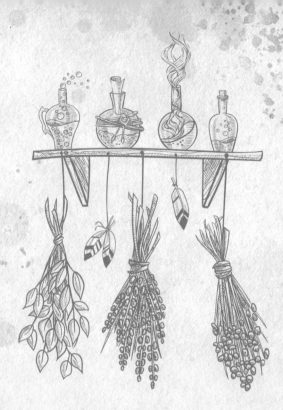

Decorating Your Fairy Altar

Your fairy altar will evolve along with your magical practice.
Decorating your altar is a personal choice. Cover your altar with a
cloth if you wish—maybe in a color that represents your intentions.
As much as possible, keep the elements that make up your altar
natural, for their innate individual energies.

Before decorating, physically cleaning the space where your altar
resides removes negative energy and makes space for good vibes
to flourish—which will encourage the fairies to bloom (they are
particular about neatness and order). Wipe it clean with rosemary
water or rose water. Sweep it clean with a bundle of lavender
blooms. Ceremonially cleaning your space can be an alternative.
Consider a besom broom or common sage cleansing spray to help
whisk away any energy that does not serve.

On your altar, you may wish to include any or all of the following, but always do what feels right to you and is true to your heart:

- Representations of the fairies you seek, such as pictures, statues, or sacred flowers.

- Water, whether charged by the Full Moon's light and a fairy's blessing, or sourced from a river, stream, or ocean, for cleansing and blessing your altar.

- A bowl of clean soil, Himalayan salt, crystals, or seeds to represent the element of Earth and all you admire about the Fairies' Realm.

- Candles in colors that support your intentions, or use colored crystal candleholders with white candles in their place, or tealight candles to set the space atwinkle.

- Fairy lights hung in your space, or strings of white lights to decorate your altar and set the mood.

- Crystals whose vibrational energies connect with your goals and resonate with you, or are particular favorites of the fairies (see page 105).

- A fairy wand crafted from a found twig or branch that crossed your path.

- Essential oils to incorporate into spellwork or rituals, or for use in mediation.

- Pictures of loved ones, or other reminders of those important to you.

- Fairy tarot cards, rune tiles, a small cauldron, scrying bowl, or other tools to assist in daily meditation, intention setting, or spellwork.

- Dried herbs, fresh flowers, or other plants, such as hawthorn blossoms—adored by the fairies—to reflect your intentions and add an element of natural beauty to celebrate and magnify the energies your soul seeks and honor the fairy spirits.

- Books that have special meaning, including a journal.

- Bells, chimes, or singing bowl to center the mind and add the joy of fairy music.

- A mini wishing well to collect your fairy wishes.

- Found things—they're gifts from the fairies.

FAIRY CRYSTALS

Fairies love sparkle, and crystals and their sparkling energy are a natural companion to fairy magic. They not only help you attract the fairies' attention and signal your openness to communicate, but can also help manifest your intentions with an extra energy boost to support what the fairies offer and let you tap into their wisdom and lessons.

- **Amethyst** boosts intuition, making it easier to detect the fae's presence. Amethyst can also help you strengthen relationships, fairy or otherwise, and offers a strong healing, calming energy and an element of spiritual protection.

- **Angel aura crystal** is protective and soothing. This crystal has the power to connect you with your spirit guide, who just may be in the form of a fairy (see page XX). Angel aura crystal promotes loving communication with anyone in your life.

- **Aquamarine** gives us the courage to face what life throws our way with an ease and go-with-the-flow attitude. Place aquamarine in a glass of clean water on your altar or in a water feature in your garden to signal to any water fairy your desire to talk.

⚬ **Celestite**, with its heavenly blue hue, guarantees messages from the angelic fairies. Use to support meditation when seeking tranquility or divine guidance.

⚬ **Citrine**, with its sunny optimism, helps clarify thoughts when choices are required and manifests abundance, which increases gratitude and generosity—traits the fairy folk love and admire. Citrine's lively energy is also said to protect against malevolent fairies. Keep one around until you get to know your new fairy friends.

⚬ **Fairy quartz**, this sparkling crystal, possesses a gentle, soothing energy for healing meditation, and it eases emotional pain and stress. It facilitates intuitive and heightened communication with fairy friends, and lifts the energy and spirit of those around it. Place fairy quartz under your pillow and invite the fairies to visit your dreams.

⚬ **Green jade** brings wealth, prosperity, and extreme good luck. Increase your luck in making the acquaintance of the magical fae with this charming crystal in hand.

- **Moldavite**, literally *born of the stars*, is among the rarest of materials on Earth. This highly vibrational crystal resulted from a huge meteorite collision with Earth about fifteen million years ago. The Czech Republic, near the Moldau River (hence moldavite's name), is the single source of this transformative stone. If you are lucky enough to have some, its energies are said to bring healing, particularly connecting mind and heart, enhance intuitive abilities, and effect swift change. All those beings not of this realm are attracted to moldavite. Joining forces with the fae, moldavite can help reveal the true purpose for our time on Earth.

- **Prehnite**, with its earthy green color, provides special energy to attract fairies and is said to enhance your prophetic senses, such as clairvoyance and claircognizance. Its energies will help align yours with Nature, and bring you closer to the compassionate Fairy Realm. Prehnite also offers an orb of protective energy from random encounters with evil fairies. Used in meditation, prehnite keeps you grounded in the present.

- **Rainbow aura quartz**, placed in the garden, can offer a lovely place for a fairy to check their reflection and radiate joy throughout your space as you work to manifest your fairy dreams.

- **Rainbow moonstone**, with its rainbow-hued shimmer, may be just the portal entry you need to Fairyland. Said to be born of the moonbeams, and thus of the Moon, its energies are naturally connected to water and the water fairies. As a stone of new beginnings, it may be just the signal your new fairy friend needs to make an approach.

- **Rose quartz**, the crystal of boundless unselfish love, will boost your abilities to love yourself and others unconditionally and attract the gentle fairy souls to you.

- **Tourmaline**, and all its sparkly beauty, is a powerful fairy crystal and definitely appeals to the fae and their magical chemistry. Black tourmaline can provide a shield of protection around you. Green tourmaline, when buried in a garden or flowerpot, encourages lush, healthy plants to bloom and its power can connect you to the Nature fairies and their elemental and healing magic. A green tourmaline wand is sure to conjure fairy company and the blessings of their charms. Pink tourmaline can help you communicate with the angelic fairies. Watermelon tourmaline, with its fascinating combination of the energies of both green and pink tourmaline and which looks like a sweet treat attractive to the fae, draws beneficial spirits to you while empowering you to rid your life of anything preventing the manifestation of your goals. Honor the magical workings of the fairies in all aspects of your life by keeping tourmaline on your fairy altar or wearing it in celebration of your magical powers.

◌ **Turquoise** may help facilitate communication with the fae because its calming properties allow the mind to focus, which fosters clearer thinking and communication. Its lovely blue color and association with both air and water, make turquoise the perfect stone for seeking the company of Undines and Sylphs.

FAIRY STONES

Like other crystals you may choose to work your fairy magic with, fairy stones create a constant energy flow connecting you with the fae for magical work.

◌ Fairy stones in the shape of disks are interesting calcium carbonate mineral deposits often formed around small pebbles and can be found in Canada and the British Isles among other places. Sometimes called goddess stones because of their resemblance to the female form, they are also used to enhance fertility magic or boost your fairy goddess charms.

◌ Fairy stones in the shape of crosses (St. Andrew's) are formed from staurolite and can be found across the United States (especially in Virginia). Their origins are said to be the fairies' tears on learning of the death of Christ.

- Fairy stones with holes in them, also called hag's stones—are said to be the key to entering Fairyland: Close one eye, peer through the hole, and fairies you'll spy; depending on where you find your stone, you may meet water fairies or forest fairies attuned to its magic.

- Other fairy stones are stones you're just drawn to, or directed to by your fairy guide.

All fairy stones also have a powerful connection with Earth and her healing energies and bring good luck and offer protection from negative energies—and evil spirits—as well as call wealth and abundance to you. They provide an immense sense of grounding, while at the same time they can connect your mind and heart to the spirit realm. Giving fairy stones as gifts strengthens your bond with the receiver and is like passing on a bit of luck. The most powerful fairy stones for help working with the fae are the ones you find yourself. Carry, wear, or use fairy stones in meditation when working with the fairies for magical outcomes.

FAIRY STAR

The number seven has various spiritual meanings attached to it that go back through centuries, cultures, and religions. Examples include the Pleiades or Seven Sisters, the seven classical planets, the seven days of the week, and the seven days of creation. This seven-pointed symbol, drawn in a single line, known as the fairy star, faery star, or elven star, is used frequently to represent the world of the fae in Pagan traditions and is thought to be a portal to the Otherworld.

When compared to the five-pointed pentacle, with its points corresponding to earth, air, fire, water, and Spirit (or above) and which is said to represent elemental magic, the fairy star represents the magic of the heavens, or realms other than Earth, and correspondingly its points mirror the pentacle's with the addition of *below* and *within*, those unseen realms shrouded in mystery.

Use this guiding symbol in meditation when contacting the Fairy Realm, while spellcasting, or as a signal that the fae are welcome—but use it wisely and honor its power. It is said that those whose blood flows from witches or fairies are able to access its deepest power.

FAIRY DUST

Fairy dust, also called Pixie dust, is the soul of Nature and one of the most powerful tools of the fairies. It can help make good things happen, like granting wishes or the power of flight, growing lush garden plants, bestowing good health, casting circles and spells based on intentions, spreading joy, and making dreams come true. Though sparkly and shiny, it can be hard to locate and harvest in Nature, so see page 128 for some secret recipes to make your own so you're never without.

FAIRY WAND

A fairy wand is a common accessory in Fairyland, used to wield magical power and cast circles. Some say only fairy queens have wands as a status symbol, to accompany their crowns, but not everyone believes that. The best fairy wand material is young elder wood, or any young stick or limb that falls from the tree naturally. Adorn your wand with glitter, paint, sayings, dates, words, or images and top it off with your most magical crystal or a star. Feel the power.

FAIRY HERBS

In addition to the flowers, herbs, and trees noted in Planting and Tending a Fairy Garden (page 96), which are among some of the more well-known that fairies are attracted to, these herbs are particularly helpful in fairy magic work, but use what speaks to you. Herbs gathered on Midsummer's Eve are said to be at their highest energy potential.

DANDELION

For wishes granted. Wishes blown upon dandelion seeds are delivered straight to the fairies for granting.

ELDER TREE

For protection of your home. Its berries and flowers can be used to whip up a little fairy kitchen magic, such as for jams, syrups, wines, and even champagne.
To sleep under the elder is to dance among the fairies. Be kind to the tree, for damaging it will bring the wrath of the fairies upon you.

FOXGLOVE

For protection. Though purely ornamental (it's poisonous), it is a fairy favorite. Its original name, folksglove, speaks to the flowers' resemblance to the fingers of a glove and refers to the "Good Folk," the fairies who dwell deep within the forest where "folksglove" grew. Its bell-shaped flowers can be heard tolling if you have fairies living amongst your herbs.

HONEYSUCKLE

For love. Fairies are drawn to its tempting scent, so be sure to leave a few blossoms on the vine when harvesting it for your altar or spellwork.

LADY'S MANTLE

For powerful energy in attracting love, as well as opening our intuition pathways. The fairies delight in drinking the plant's magical dew as an elixir.

VERVAIN

For help with clairvoyance, happiness, and prosperity.

FAIRY WINGS AND MORE

Adorn yourself with fairy wings, a luscious perfume, a glittery glow, a sparkly tiara, or fairy flower crown. Don a flowing gown, step into fairy slippers, or carry a bouquet of fairy flower messages. Dive into the sea, climb a tree, stroll in the grass, or feel the wind in your hair. Paint your nails, color your lips, tint your hair. Wear no jewelry or everything you own. Choose colors you love or that make you feel safe, or empowered, or . . . magical and reflect your intentions. However you're moved, dress the part and feel yourself connect with your fairy magic. If it's good enough for the fairies, it's definitely good enough for you.

WISHES GRANTED

Some fairies are especially attuned to hearing wishes from humans and making them a reality—and if that wish is made upon a falling star, its energy travels faster through the Universe. Wishes blown on dandelion seeds are received directly by fairies for granting (see Dandelion Wishes Fairy Spell Jar, page 154). Add a little fairy magic to someone's life by granting them a special wish. It doesn't have to take a lot of time or money; a simple act of kindness or generosity for Nature or others can get the fairy wish train rolling along.

FOUND THINGS

Fairies love to "borrow" things, and those things are usually what you've misplaced or "lost"—it's a form of entertainment for them (and a source of frustration for us!). Sometimes, you're lucky enough to locate that "lost" item and sometimes it's gone for good. I think this is the tradeoff we assume when inviting these Good Folks into our world.

However, consider, instead, the "found" things that crop up in your life: bits of ribbon or string, coins, feathers, stones, brightly colored fallen leaves, animals, seashells, a new route home that invites a stop for the view—these are all gifts from the fairies and can be used to heighten your fairy magic energies. Perhaps someone somewhere just found your "lost" sunglasses . . . the fairies must know they need them more than you do to see their world more clearly. Consider what your found things may be telling you and you're likely to see their beauty and value increase accordingly. Consider the magic that just entered your world and leave an offering in return.

Create Enchantment In Your Life

Fairy magic is simple magic. As such, it does not require a lot of rite or ritual. The magical potions, meditation, rituals, and spells suggested here are merely ways to enhance your communication and provide ideas to get your messages out into the Universe where they will be heard and returned. Use these ideas as is, or make them your own. Sometimes, too, magic just happens in stillness—when you least expect it.

FAIRY FESTIVITIES

airy holidays align with the seasons and honor the cycles of the Earth, Moon, and Sun—and the heightened energies of the time are the perfect opportunity for connection. And although many who believe follow the Pagan festivals of Sabbat and Esbat, any festival important to your culture and heritage is ripe for celebration with the fairies. And, if your celebration includes special or traditional food and drink, leave a bit for the fairies so they know they're welcome.

For a boost to your fairy magic rituals, coordinate intentions and spellwork with as many appropriate celebrations, as you can.

SABBAT CELEBRATIONS

The eight Sabbats honor the Sun and the changing year—four correspond to its solstices and equinoxes, and another four to the seasons and their harvests. Combined, the Sabbats mark the Wheel of the Year, listed here as they occur in the Northern Hemisphere.

WINTER SOLSTICE (YULE)

Generally, December 21.
A time of celebration and offerings.

Give thanks to the fairies for the magical gifts and you will be blessed with good luck—a tidy nook or bit of honey or holiday cake is a good place to start.

IMBOLC

February 2.
A celebration of the Earth's reawakening.

The fairies may be stirring from a long winter's nap in anticipation of spring. A little bread and butter to greet them will be appreciated.

OSTARA

Generally, March 21.
Corresponding to spring equinox; a time of heightened fertility on Earth.

You may sense the fairies abuzz tending to the first blooms bursting forth. Wave hello!

BELTANE
May 1, May Day.
A celebration of fertility and the
impending return of summer; a time of
planting and an acknowledgment of the
cycle of birth, growth, and death.

*Look for fairies dancing among the
bluebells as they sway in rhythm to the
breeze. Early risers may learn their beauty
secrets—fairies bathe in the dew collected
in lady's mantle leaves.*

LITHA (MIDSUMMER)
Generally, June 21.
Corresponding to summer solstice when
the Sun is at its most powerful, nourishing
and nurturing Earth's crops.

*Although midsummer is the longest day of
the year, the real celebration for the fairy
folk occurs on Midsummer's Eve, when
they're believed to be most active on Earth
and, traditionally, offerings are left for
them in gratitude and appeasement.*

LAMMAS

August 1.

A celebration of early harvest and the first of three harvest Sabbats; a day of gratitude for the abundance we reap.

Fairy activity may move from the garden to the house, as house fairies bustle and tidy what's been neglected in favor of being outside.

MABON

Generally, September 21.

Corresponding with fall equinox; the second of the harvest festivals; while celebrating the life-giving qualities of Earth, we also acknowledge and plan for the darker times ahead.

If you notice those last lingering fruits and vegetables disappearing from the garden, it may not be the birds or squirrels, but the fairies storing up for winter.

SAMHAIN

October 31.

The witch's new year; a time when the veil between this world and the next is said to be its thinnest and, so, a good time to connect with loved ones who have passed and fairies in our realm; a pause in the Earth's growing cycle as she prepares to rest and renew.

Fairies seek shelter in preparation for the coming winter. You may notice a shimmering shadow as daylight grows shorter and the veil to the Otherworld thins.

ESBAT CELEBRATIONS

The energies of Esbat correspond to the energies of the Moon's phases and so there are eight, like Sabbats:

New Moon

Waxing Crescent

First Quarter Moon

Waxing Gibbous

Full Moon

Waning Gibbous

Third Quarter Moon

Waning Crescent

And although each Moon phase is ripe for celebration and fairy magic, the power of the New Moon, as that time between darkness and emerging light, is an active fairy period for communication. The Full Moon is also especially meaningful in fairy magic traditions, as our Good Neighbors are said to be particularly active then, as they revel in the Moon's full light—especially at midnight, the fairy hour.

FAIRY POTIONS

airy potions are as powerful as the fairies themselves and are used for many magical purposes, such as to attune yourself to the fairy frequency, as offerings and to welcome fairies into your world, as well as to heighten the magical energies fairies emit. Fairy potions should only be made with natural ingredients and can be tailored to your needs. Whether laughter, love, healing, sleep, or wisdom, there's a potion for that. And, if you spy one left for you by the fairies, expect it to be doubly effective!

From petals soft as morning dew with kiss of fairy's dust imbued.
This potion is a potent gift, whose powers charm at once when used.
With flick or two from fairy's wand,
the magic spreads from here beyond.
And to the sweet and kindly fae, my thanks are true, my heart is gay.
For joy and beauty left in your wake,
doth fill a soul with magic's quake.

FAIRY WATER

Water imbued with a fairy's magic can be kept on your altar as an offering. Here, we'll use a fairy favorite, the sweetly scented rose, whose intoxicating perfume tempts fairies to your garden. If you prefer the scent or have a garden abloom, you can also use organic lavender buds.

1 Choose four or five fresh, fragrant, *organic* roses (no chemicals or pesticides, please!) to create your fairy water. If you're lucky enough to have a blooming rose garden tended by the Flower Fairies, harvest the roses in morning, once the dew evaporates, when their fragrance is strongest, and honor the Rose Fairy's contribution. Otherwise, roses from your favorite florist will be fine.

2 Separate the petals from the stems—aim for about 2 heaping cups of petals (weight varies). Rinse the petals, if needed, and place them in a small pot. You can also use dried organic petals (about 1 cup).

3 Add 3 cups (720 ml) water to the pot, cover it with a lid, and bring to a boil, then reduce the heat to maintain the lowest simmer. Cook for about 10 minutes, checking after 5 minutes, or until the petals are drained of all their color. Remove from the heat and let cool completely, covered.

4 Strain the petals in a fine-mesh strainer set over a bowl, gently pressing on them to get out as much liquid as you can. Discard the petals and transfer the water to a clean bottle. Leave the water out overnight on a windowsill facing the Moon and ask the fairies to bless it with a kiss of their fairy wings. Refrigerate for 1 to 2 weeks.

FAIRY DUST

To add that special magical aura to spellwork, mealtime, or to cast a circle—not as a barrier but, rather, an invitation to the fairy folk to join you in mediation or rituals, or as an entryway to their world—fairy dust is an indispensable tool to keep stocked. It's easy to make your own. Here are three different approaches to fairy dust (all Earth-friendly, which is a requirement in the fairy world). This is also a great project for involving kids in your magical world.

To care for our Earth and the fairies, when using glitter, choose eco-friendly biodegradable glitters only. Transfer the fairy dust to small glass or plastic jars (in the spirit of eco-friendliness, reuse empty spice jars with the plastic shaker tops, baby food jars, or old salt or pepper shakers).

Create a decorative label, if you wish, and store until you're ready to use.

NOTE: You may be tempted to add salt to Nature's Fairy Dust or swap salt for sugar in Fairy Dust Sprinkle: Don't. Fairies detest salt.

Of sparkle and glow, as above so below.
I urge you, "Set sail," down this fairy dust trail,
For it leads to a place full of magical grace
Where friendship does flow from the first word: hello.

Nature's Fairy Dust

Scatter this fairy dust outside freely to honor the fairies and send messages using the language of herbs and flowers.

1 Place 1 cup (or more based on how much fairy dust you want) of rice or birdseed into a large bowl. In smaller amounts based on your preference, stir in any or all of the following dried herbs and flowers, or add others you prefer:

- **Bay leaf:** for invitation and good wishes
- **Caraway:** for fine health
- **Chamomile:** for soothing sleep
- **Cinnamon:** for abundance
- **Dill:** to keep harm from the fairies
- **Hibiscus:** for enhanced intuition
- **Holy basil (tulsi):** for serenity

- **Hops:** for sweet dreams
- **Lavender:** for peace
- **Nutmeg:** for luck
- **Oregano:** for courage
- **Parsley:** for gratitude
- **Rosemary:** for honor and loyalty
- **Rose petals:** for love
- **Sage:** for wisdom
- **Sweet pea:** for friendship
- **Violet:** for creativity

2 Add color and shine with a glitter or two of choice—as much or as little as you like. Stir and get ready to celebrate the fairies.

FAIRY DUST SPRINKLE

This edible fairy dust can add magic to mealtimes as well as spell times. Sprinkle on toast, ice cream, whipped cream, cookies, cereal, marshmallows, or decorate a piecrust; rim a cocktail glass or an iced-tea glass; use as a dip for fresh fruit, if you like. You may even want to make multiple smaller batches in different colors to combine, or choose colors based on the type of fairy you are befriending (blue for water fairies, green for Earth fairies, pink for flower fairies, etc.)—sprinkle lightly on top of a glass of milk left as an offering!

1   In a large bowl, combine granulated sugar—the amount depends on how much fairy dust you want—with food coloring of choice (start with a few drops and add more to achieve the color you like). Thoroughly whisk the sugar and coloring to blend until uniform throughout.

2   Spread the sugar on a rimmed baking sheet and bake in a 350°F (180°C) oven for 8 to 10 minutes to set the color.

3   Remove and let cool completely, before breaking up any sugar clumps and storing.

FAIRY DUST SPARKLE

Use (and, preferably, make) this fairy dust outside to add beauty and glittering effects to any fairy celebration. Remember, fairies love all things shiny!

1   In a large mixing bowl, mix two or three different colors of extra-fine glitter, like blue and silver, or purple and pink—the amounts depend on how much fairy dust you want.

2   Stir in other types and textures of glitter, as you like, for fun and extra sparkle—look for glow-in-the-dark glitter for those Moonlight celebrations. Keep stored in a container with a tight-fitting lid when not in use.

FAIRY MAGIC BOOSTERS

Friends do things for friends to make them feel loved, welcome, appreciated, and noticed. Do the same for your fairy friends. Be sure to incorporate some natural element that is particularly meaningful to the fairies you're communicating with (and not just about your intentions) each time you seek their company or guidance. Candles for the fire fairies; a feather for the air fairies, crystals for Earth elementals; essential oil for Flower Fairies and tree spirits make it feel like home; water features attract all fairies; found things are fairy gifts to you and using them will delight the fae.

FAIRY MEDITATIONS

Being "on the same page" with someone feels good: It demonstrates agreement and empathy and validates your thoughts and feelings. A walkabout with Nature and her animal companions can be your chance to be on the same page with the Fairy Realm and offers a splendid way to attune to the fairies around you.

ATTUNING TO NATURE MEDITATION— THE FAIRIES' REALM

This guided Nature walk can be done from the comfort of your chair using the power of your mind's eye, but if you are able to take it outside to harness the uplifting power that Nature offers, feel free to do so. This visualization can be your time to feel grounded, or energized, or both, to attune to your magical powers and explore the concept of opening your heart and mind to new experiences. A conversation with Nature is therapy of the finest kind. A fairy companion or two along the way blesses you with magic, indeed.

- Take a deep, cleansing breath, in and out, being fully aware of your breath. Focus on how your body feels as it breathes in healing oxygen and releases any stress or tension on the exhale. Visualize your tense muscles relaxing and feel yourself become lighter as a result. Listen for the quiet. Breathe until you feel fully present in the moment, with no worries on your mind.

As you continue to breathe, imagine you're in a soothing, friendly forest with trees (and Tree Fairies) of all sorts towering over a garden path. Look around you. Look up. Look down. Notice the details that delight.

As you begin to walk the path, you spot a beautiful blooming garden in the distance. But, first, notice the trees that line the pathway. Attune to their spirit: Can you hear their leaves rustle? What are they saying? Do the trees provide shade or are you walking in sunshine because the leaves have fallen? Is the air cool, damp, warm, or dry? Can you feel the energy of the wind on your face? Do you spy a fairy door? Do you hear fairy chatter—maybe the buzzing of bees or the scamper of squirrels? Stop for a moment to enjoy the sensations. Can you smell the Pine Tree Fairy welcoming you? What other trees stand guard along the path? Feel their energy fill your heart.

Are birds singing in the trees—perhaps there are fairy songs mixed in? Listen for a moment to find a call and response . . . that pair of birds is watching over you.

As you continue along the path, how does the ground feel beneath your feet? Is the path smooth? Rocky? Gnarled with tree roots? With each step, connect to the Earth's energy and the Earth Fairies tending this path. Feel the energy charge through your leg muscles and up into your torso, increasing your pace toward the garden where fairies of all types are sure to reside. Give thanks to Earth for her support in all things and pledge to work with the fairies to continue to sustain her.

As you emerge from the forest and get closer to the garden, what other plants, herbs, or flowers can you see? Blooming clover nodding cheerfully? An overgrown rose bush beckoning with its scent? A mossy step? A Jack-in-the pulpit? Willows waving hello? Which bloom profusely, indicating a fairy's tender care?

Attune your ears to the babbling brook. Stop for a minute to listen to the brook laughing with its Water Fairy inhabitants as it trips along its bed. Bend down to put a hand in the water. Feel its cooling energy against your skin. The garden calls, but you're in no hurry. All is good. You are here. It is joy. Breathe and believe.

When you're ready, continue along to the garden. It's in full bloom and the energy and scents are intoxicating. Which scents can you identify? Have you felt the flit of a fairy wing near your cheek?

- Continue to walk through the garden, visualizing all your favorite plants as you go. Stop along the way to smell, taste, touch, and feel thoroughly connected to your garden. Feel the Sun on your face—the touch of a Fire Fairy. What do you say to the plants? What do they say to you? Take a moment to appreciate the garden fairies for the bounty and the beauty and energy this garden gives your life.

- It's time to return home—don't worry; you can come back here any time you like. On the journey home, relive the peaceful, nurturing, connecting emotions you felt to the forest, the garden, and all the fairies within. Can you sense why the fairies are at home here? Can you hear them whispering to you to come back? Delight in the possibilities. You are attuned to the Fairy Realm.

FLYING FREELY—FAIRY MEDITATION
TO EASE STRESS

airies are creatures of habit and they like things
"just so" . . . orderly, stress-free, and joyful. When your mind
feels a bit jumbled and your universe is swirling in chaos, it's time
to summon fairy energy to negate the stress and soothe the soul
so you can recoup your fairy magic pronto. Open the door to invite
fairies in and usher stress out.

- Sitting comfortably and quietly, outside in the Fairy Realm
  preferably, where you can engage all your senses among their
  world, gather your intentions: to be relaxed, ease away stress,
  clear the storms in your mind, and embrace a sense of beauty
  and ease in which to live. Breathe in deeply, hold, and breathe
  out fully. Repeat and relax until you feel ready to begin.

- Call on your fairy friends to join you. Believe they will hear you
  and oblige. You may sense them before you see them (if you do
  see them at all!). Hear the tinkle of their bells, or their laugh.
  Their wings beat slowly—feel the kiss of their breeze. Give your
  wings a stretch. Sudden sweet aromas of the fields and flowers
  are a sure sign they're near. See them sitting next to you,
  forming a circle of glittering, sparkling light. Their auras shine
  brilliantly. Feel the peace.

- Join hands, and say quietly or aloud:

*May the peace and love encircled here fill me with light
that I may open my heart to all who share my plight.
When chaos threatens to overwhelm my sight
with fairy wings, I lift myself into serene flight.*

As you continue to breathe fully in and release any stress or fear on the out-breath, feel the weight of your worries releasing from your body. Feel the relief the lightness brings. Let it ease you from your seat as you see yourself taking flight, feeling the wind beneath your wings, floating high—now, soaring above it all as an observer. See the beauty and expanse. You are not affected by the stress and strain, but feel only peace at being above it all. Feel the lightness of your true heart sailing through the skies, singing with the wind. Feel the lift created by the fairies flying with you—their wings lifting you higher.

Float freely. Relax. Feel the rush of the wind washing away any last bits of stress. Feel the warmth of the Sun nurturing your soul and unfurling your wings. Hear the songs of the birds welcoming you. Feel empowered to handle anything. Feel joy knowing you can direct the outcome however you wish. Realize you are so far above Earth that you cannot even see what was troubling you. Let it go.

Visualize fairy dust being released from your wings, and those of the fairies around you, as they beat to keep you aloft, covering everything with an ethereal glow. The beauty leaves you in awe. Absorb the feeling, that you may come back to it when needed. Stay here as long as you need.

When ready, ask the fairies to help glide you to Earth. Wiggle your toes, stretch your arms, and fold your fairy wings. Smell the grass, winds, flowers, trees. Feel Earth beneath you. Alight on a flower and let yourself feel the soft landing and sweet, welcoming scents. Inhale. Exhale. Open your eyes, if they are closed. Feel the lightness in your body and the sparkle in your heart. The fairies were here with you.

Acknowledge their presence and leave a gift in their honor. Carry on in the peace and calm of the Fairy Realm.

FAIRY SPELLS AND RITUALS

airy spells and rituals can be as simple or elaborate as you are comfortable doing, or are inspired to do. They offer a way to organize your intentions and, thus, their communication to the fairies for help and the Universe to respond. Instant results are never guaranteed, practice and patience are surely required, but never doubt your magic or your power. When linked with the enchantment of the fae and the energies of the Universe, your true intentions will sparkle and your dreams will manifest when they align with your true heart.

FAIRIES AND WITCHES

It is said that the fairies teach witches how to create and cast spells. There is much to learn from these kindred spirits, whose powers and pleasures can enhance our own.

ABUNDANCE AND SUCCESS

Growing Wealth

The Earth as an element represents many things, including wealth and abundance, and it grounds us in the reality of the work needed to achieve our goals. Achieving abundance in material wealth is possible with the assist of the Earth fairies, but they can be a temperamental bunch, so approach with caution and deference. Some of the most helpful allies to seek help from include the Dwarves and Gnomes, or the Tree or Flower Fairies.

A circle cast with mugwort, honeysuckle, or primrose can be an invitation to the fae. Cast this spell at dawn or dusk, that in-between time, when fairy activity can be at its peak, outside, if possible, and leave the patch of Earth you choose to work with in better shape than you found it as an offering. When ready, say quietly or aloud:

I touch the Earth to honor her and all that she creates.
I listen for the fairies hard at work within her core,
who tend and guard and work so hard, to keep her spirit fed.
I ask a boost of energy from them to bind with mine,
that fertile may my efforts be—that wealth begins to shine.

Blooming Friendships

Water Fairies, with their energies devoted to harmony and tranquility, and their natural attunement to emotions, can be the perfect bridge to developing new friendships. Incorporating the element of water into this spell, whether fairy water to bless your altar, fresh water to tend to your fairy garden, or a cup of herbal tea (one for you; one for your fairy friend)—apple, passionflower, or rose for close friendship—will signal the fairies' attention and help the flow of communication begin. When ready, say quietly or aloud:

Friendship that flows with love and grace as streams
through vibrant lands,
new seedlings, new roots, new branches,
new shoots to blossom where empty ground stands.
Companions I seek, whose hearts open wide,
with whom to join hand in hand.
Please bless me, dear fairies, with sprinkles of dew
that new friends bloom strong and true.

Career Change

We know that fairies pursue careers and pastimes just like we do, and like humans, even when you find something you're good at or enjoy, the glow can sometimes dim, and you can feel a little stuck in a rut. And although humans fear change, fairies possess the ability to see farther into the future than we do and, therefore, can appreciate the advantages of something new and the growth it nurtures. When you think you may have outgrown your current job, or crave a career change to pursue your heart's desire, call on your fairy board of directors for a little help and direction. When ready to begin the meeting, or meditation, say quietly or aloud:

I thank this glorious group for convening here today,
to prep me for the interviews that open new doorways.
For once inside, your fairy lore and wisdom will ignite—
then, passion to reveal my true and sparkling self takes flight.
On fairy wings I hope to land the job that will delight.

Firefly Fairy Freedom

Fairies are most active at those in-between times, like dusk. Is it any coincidence, then, that fireflies begin their wondrous show at dusk as well? These enchanting "Fire Fairies" ignite wonder and joy in us all. They light the way in darkness and reveal our true path. These fairy companions illuminate our souls and remind us to stay true to ourselves. They teach us that our light shines brightest when it burns freely—and attracts likeminded energies. Invite a child along for the fun. When ready to light up your world, say quietly or aloud:

Each firefly I see tonight bears fairy dust to spread delight.
I join the fairies in their dance and revel in sweet freedom's chance
to burn as brightly as I dare, for fairy truth has brought me here.
On fairy wings I'll travel free, in search of just what I can be.

Luck of the Fairies

Irish lore says the luck of the Irish belongs to the fairies and it is they, those Good Folk, who dole it out as they see fit—but currying their favor can sometimes seem like a full-time job in itself. With appropriate offerings and attention, however, the Four-Leaf Clover Fairy, or any of his lucky friends, may be open to your request for a charmed lucky break. When ready, say quietly or aloud:

Your buttered bread and water wait, the fire smolders tight.
The house is clean, the horses fed, the barn secured for night.
These offerings I make, dear fae,
in hopes you'll throw some luck my way.
A sign from you will make my day—a signal luck is mine this day.

New Moon / New Intentions

The New Moon is the start of the Moon's monthly cycle and its
waxing phases—and a prime time to enter the Fairy Realm. It
is especially a time of new beginnings and a time to set new
intentions to achieve our dreams. Although still a time of darkness,
it is our belief in what we cannot see, but know to be true, that
perseveres. Call on the Moon Fairies to ignite curiosity, wonder, and
enchantment, to help plant the seeds of intentions that grow into
wishes granted. Align your true wishes with the truth of your heart
and, when ready, say quietly or aloud:

New light, new view, new time, new glow,
new wishes dreamed, intentions grow.
Moon Fairy show your Moonlit face,
enchant my world with fairy grace.
Unsure of where this path will lead,
I take you hand in trust indeed
to lead me to my heart's desire
intentions blessed, may you inspire.

New Horizons

Although staying close to home definitely has its perks, especially when you've got your fairy friends for company and to help with chores, traveling—near or afar—teaches us so much and gives us the magical opportunity to spread our fairy wings and test their resilience. When the chance to travel presents itself, seek guidance from the fae for smooth sailing dusted with a little wonder along the way and say quietly or aloud:

From fairy dreams my wishes grow to flit and fly and journey so.
This wanderlust that fills my heart is but the seed with which to start.
Dear fae, do take me on your wings that soar and dip and sweetly sing
of the beauty that is Fairyland, with maps and plans,
we're hand in hand—
for changed we'll be upon new shores, where hopes and
dreams are what's in store.

New Home Sweet Home

When shopping for a new home, you likely have a list of needs and wants. Consider what your fairy friends need, too, in order to feel welcome and at home in the new space (assuming they're traveling with you)—and to help maintain a peaceful atmosphere. Spend a few quiet minutes in meditation, asking your fairy companions to join and make known their priorities for new living quarters and for help locating just the right place. When ready, say quietly or aloud:

This house we'll call home will be open and free,
to shelter and love and create family.
Where peace reigns supreme and love rules the day,
this house will be perfect for mortals and fae.
The signs that I seek are the flowers that bloom all over
the yard and within each new room.
This place will be ours, there's no need to roam—
your blessings have found us our new home sweet home.

Selling a Home

Sometimes, selling a home means leaving behind the many fairy friends you've found, those unable to move with you, like the Gnomes, Flower Fairies and Water Fairies, or Tree Spirits . . . even that household helper may prefer to stay. Help the sale go smoothly by enlisting the help of the fairies in picking the perfect buyer.

You may want to start with an herbal smoke cleanse, to clear any existing negative history of the home. Then, when ready, say quietly or aloud:

Fairy magic bright and strong, charm sweet buyers with your song.
Entice the ones you'd like to stay and (nicely) lead the rest astray.
This home is yours, but time has come,
to welcome new friends—and then some.
Bless this house, may bluebells bloom,
where fairies' laughter welcomes you.

Crystal Fairy Blooms

Once fairies are settled into your gardens, they love nothing more than tending the plants and blooms. Signs of fairy inhabitation will be evident everywhere you look. That said, they do appreciate a little help and some added sparkle when you can. Add these crystals to your garden, and any others you wish (see page 105 for some ideas), and offer a little spell of thanks, to encourage enchanting blooms all season long:

- **Clear quartz fairy water**, the all-purpose healer—clear quartz's high vibrational energy stimulates growth and will promote healing of any plants in need. Place clear quartz in your watering can (it is water-safe), fill the can with water, and let sit overnight in the garden where the fairies will imbue it with their special powers. Water your plants as needed, leaving a little of the crystal water in the can before refilling it. Clear quartz placed in the garden will boost the energies of other crystals nearby.

Moss agate, the gardener's stone, enhances your connection with Earth and promotes a healthy, lush garden. This crystal is perfect for adorning fairy gardens, or any garden, and will appeal to all the Nature Fairies, attracting them—and abundance—into your life.

When ready, say quietly or aloud:

Elements of Nature bring,
your powers forth to make Earth sing.
To laugh in blooms that dance with ease
and catch the sighs of whispering trees.
Where fairies are at work and play,
a garden's blooms forever stay.
I'm blessed with bounty from the fae;
these crystals shine my thanks your way.

Fairy Sleep

We need it. We crave it. We fret about not having it—calm, serene, restful sleep. It's the stuff that dreams are made of. When the sweet sleep of fairies eludes—you or the kids—skip the lullabies and go straight to the source: Mr. Sandman, a.k.a. the Sleep Fairy. His charms are too tough to resist and a visit from him means you'll soon be snoozing in the flower-filled Fairyland of your dreams. When ready to enter dreamland, get comfortable in bed, relax your mind, and say quietly or aloud:

The lights are low, the pillows fluffed, the covers are just right.
There's room for you, it's comfy too, please join me here tonight.
For sleep's the plan and you're the man
to make my dreams come true—
a sprinkle of your magic dust is all I need from you.
Please, Sandman, wave your magic wand that
sleep lasts sweet all night.

Baby's Blessing

It's said the fairies, especially Fairy Godmothers, appear at christenings to bestow gifts on newborns to bless them for life. What more delightful way to enter this world than to be kissed by the fairies, completely enveloped in innocence and charm. For any newborn in your world, or in the world at large, seek the blessings these blossoming humans so richly deserve. When ready, say quietly or aloud:

On Fairy wings sweet blessings bring,
this babe in arms can hear you sing.
Dear Flower Fairies gather near and offer gifts of faith so dear.
And fairies from the stars above, do bless this babe with gifts of love.
Sweet fae from lands we've never seen,
bestow this child with wonder keen.
And Nature's spirit entourage, reveal your secrets to great courage.
And every day this child lives, may gifts of joy these fairies give.
With grateful heart and love, indeed, it's health that's asked for last,
Godspeed.

Fairy Prescription for Well-Being

Take a cue from the fairies when it comes to maintaining your well-being—physical, spiritual, and mental. Following their prescription for daily maintenance will keep you operating in tip-top shape—able to face anything and live a joyful, open life. A word of gratitude for the example shown will be appreciated.

- BE SELFISH WITH SELF-CARE: Take frequent aura-cleansing, relaxing baths. Meditate. Move. Grow. Breathe. Indulge yourself.

- **KEEP UP APPEARANCES:** Reapply that fairy sparkle as needed.

- **HAVE FUN:** Sing, dance, laugh, live, wear something shiny!

- **FALL IN LOVE:** With anything . . . a child's laugh, a falling star, a cuddly pet, a true love, a gentle breeze, blooming flowers.

- **BANISH STRESS:** Just say no.

- **SPREAD YOUR WINGS:** Try something new, just because.

- **LIVE IN THE MOMENT:** Stop, look around, see the beauty that surrounds you, feel the joy of a deep cleansing breath.

- **CELEBRATE NATURE:** It's the ultimate mood lifter.

- **PAY IT FORWARD:** Do good for the sake of good—don't expect reward, recognition, or payment in return.

- **LISTEN TO YOUR HEART:** It knows what's true.

Then, when ready, say quietly or aloud:

With humble grace I honor all the fairy ways
that teach us how to live this life enchanted and unfazed.
To be my fairy best each day, I celebrate these gifts—
that each alone seems simple, but combined are truly rich.

Inner Peace

Fairies do not like stress or chaos, preferring the soothing spirit of Nature's sights and scents. Channel your inner fairy when stress starts to wear you down and be mindful of the choice you have when reacting to it. A simple offering and a few words in prayer can put the healing energies in motion to restore your inner balance. And, when your energy shifts into a calmer state, so does the energy around you—healing a piece of the world with it.

While this spell can be done anywhere, outside among Nature and her soothing energies provides the best results to calm frustrations, or just try holding your most soothing crystal while inhaling your favorite scent. When ready, close your eyes, if you are comfortable, imagine the joyful sparkle of fairy dust surrounding you, and say quietly or aloud:

In humble need I stand before the Fairy Kingdom Realm,
With hopes you'll soothe and comfort me with all your fairy charms.
With fairy dust and fairy wand, a flourish to dispel.
Restore my inner peace at once; becalm my inner storm.

Welcoming a New Pet to the Family

Fairies love animals, and like humans, love pets—but theirs are bumblebees, inchworms, ladybugs, and caterpillars! What better helper could there be than an animal-loving fairy to have by your side when welcoming a new pet into your home and teaching it to be on its best behavior? Dogs, especially, are thought to be able to sense or see fairies. With their keen senses of sight and smell, and extraordinary ability to notice when routines change, dogs can definitely sense things we might not be attuned to. Your fairy and your furry friend just might form the tightest bond of all.

When ready to call on that special fairy to help tend to your new pet, hold the animal closely, sending all your love and good intentions for its happy life into it, feel its warmth and love in return, and say quietly or aloud:

The love between a human and the pet we pledge to love,
is nothing short of a miracle that's sent from up above.
The fairies can't help giggle when they watch how hard we try,
to speak the new pet's language but are met with vacant eyes.
So, fairy friends do enter here and make your talents known,
for speaking to the animals seems a skill that's yours alone.
I'll know you've been successful when I call, "Come, here!" and get
a fairy-dusted welcome from my fairy-trained new pet.

DANDELION WISHES FAIRY SPELL JAR

*Wishes, whether for love or other, blown on dandelion seed heads
are known to go straight into the inbox of the wish-granting fairies.
Make a dandelion wishes spell jar for even longer-lasting energy to
bring your dearest wishes to life. Place the jar in your fairy garden, on
your fairy altar, or in a window that catches the Sun's light to let your
intentions be known. Be sure to thank the plants as you harvest them
and the fairies for tending them.*

Gather:

- Fern cuttings

- Small glass jar with a lid or stopper

- Clear quartz crystal or other crystal that represents your wishes
  (such as rose quartz for love, citrine for wealth, etc.)

- Dandelion seed heads, or thistledown if you can't
  find dandelions

- Matches or a lighter

- Green candle

1 Place the fern in the jar—it will boost the magical energy—and
  place the crystal on top. Then, fill the jar with the dandelion
  seed heads.

2 Sit for a moment, holding the jar, visualizing your wishes coming
  true and imbuing the contents of the jar with energy. Secure the
  lid on the jar.

3 Light the candle and carefully drip the melting candlewax over the lid and around its edges to seal the jar. Extinguish the candle. When ready to place your jar, say quietly or aloud:

With dandelion wishes I beseech the fairies who rejoice
in bringing true a heart's delight and lending hopes a voice.
Do hear my plea, grant wishes three, spreading fairy love and joy.

4 Leave the jar sealed until your wishes are granted, then cleanse the crystal and carefully burn the plant matter in the jar or add it to a compost pile.

COMMUNICATION

Crystal Clear Intuition

A heightened psychic sense of intuition makes it easier to identify and communicate with the Wee Folk in your world. They will generally make themselves known to you on their terms, but being able to sense they're around can give you a heads-up to be receptive to and aware of their messages. Adding crystals to your spells can definitely help boost your intuitive powers and their sparkling energies will attract the fae's attention. Repeat as needed to build your "clair" or psychic senses (see page 87), as well as your creativity.

Amethyst, aquamarine, celestite, citrine, iolite, labradorite, lapis lazuli, prehnite, and rainbow moonstone, among many others, are all trusted crystals for intuitive work.

Hold a crystal in your hand, sit quietly at your fairy altar or somewhere quiet and peaceful, outside among Nature, if possible, for a moment to calm your thoughts, and, when ready, say quietly or aloud:

Crystal strength reveal to me the secret world I long to see.
Open wide my mind and heart to Fairy Realms and magic's part.
Shield me with your energy that safe from harm my journey be.
Fae, approach me gently. I wait with trusting honesty.

Sit quietly, with eyes closed if you are comfortable, for five to ten minutes, letting thoughts, sensations, sounds, and aromas surround you. What fairy messages did you intuit? Trust your intuition.

Contacting Fairies

When you've done any and all prep you want to make sure the fairies know they're welcome, such as tending your garden, setting an extra place for fairy tea or happy hour, decorating your fairy altar, or just generally tidying up, it's time to try to connect. Remember, the fairies will reveal themselves only when they're ready and comfortable doing so, meaning patience and pure intention are required on your end. When ready, say quietly or aloud:

Invited are my fairy friends, and those I've yet to meet.
To join along in joyous song, and harmonies so sweet.
With faithful heart and child's eye, I hope to see you here.
I ask you fairies, one and all, reveal yourselves to me.

Speak Your Truth

Fairies are known to be straight shooters when it comes to communication: They say what they mean and they take what you say literally—so you better mean what *you* say (there's no room for subtlety or subtext here)! Sometimes, it's hard for us to speak our truth to others but we are all better off when communication is clear, truthful, and transparent. In those times when saying what you mean, and believing in your heart, could use a little help, call on the fairies' simplest tenet to help support your message. Any blue crystal, said to help clear the throat chakra, can be paired with this spell for added clarification. When you're ready to say what you mean (and, always in a helpful way), call to your fairy spirit guide and say quietly or aloud:

Fairies come near and listen to me:
With truth in my heart, my intent is to be
as clear with my words as I am with my deeds
that all those who know me, will know what I mean.

....

Beltane Fairy Revelry

Beltane, May 1, is a special day for spending with the fairies and
living among the joy they spread—a day to let your fairy hair down,
so to speak, and be among kindred spirits and work a little magic.
Beltane is a time, like Samhain, when the veil between worlds is
at its thinnest. Unlike Samhain (where the thinning veil is said to
facilitate communication with loved ones who've passed), Beltane
has a more celebratory feel, as the world is beginning to bloom from
its winter slumber, and allows us to step closer to the Otherworld,
the land of the fairies. So, as it is a party, bring an offering, string up
some fairy lights, set up a few fairy-size tables and chairs, set your
magical intentions, and get ready to dance. When ready to reach out
to welcome the fairies, say quietly or aloud:

As Earth springs into bloom again, and all of Nature wakes,
I honor fairies' gifts bestowed just for Nature's sake.
To recognize this special time, please step into my realm, to revel,
dance, and merry make 'til dawn
does take the helm.
What magic brews within this space and time we spend as one,
will bless us with enchanting grace and secrets shared with none.

Bewitching Spell

Some in the fairy kingdom are known for their tempting, beguiling ways. Others are simply unforgettable due to their sparkle and glow, some have the personality of a charmer, and others can trick us into seeing what's not really there. Whoever your fairy inspiration is, there is no lack of irresistible energy to summon when you want to be bewitching. Take a moment to visualize yourself as you desire, summoning all your glamor and feeling the energy of attraction drawing people to you, and then, say quietly or aloud:

O' teacher of bewitching nights, do share with me your winsome rites.
Of greatest lore your charms are told to tempt, beguile with love so bold.
I wish to lure my own beloved, with Siren song and beauty coveted.
Please spin your fairy web 'round me that mesmerizing I may be.

Rose Petal Love Message

Because the Flower Fairies inhabit the particular flowers they guard and take on their flower's personality and language, we know the Rose Flower Fairy is filled with love. For a good cause, this charming fairy will eagerly donate her petal-shaped wings from each rose bloom to spread messages of love everywhere they're strewn. Think weddings, honeymoons, proposals, baby showers, birthdays, anniversaries, or any reason you have to celebrate love. Please ask permission before plucking the petals from the flower, then freely scatter wherever their messages can entice and delight. When ready to spread your fairy love wings, say quietly or aloud:

*These petals seem just a rose—though lovely on their own—
bear messages of love to each and every one they're thrown.
Look closely, etched in fairy ink, each winged message from the heart
is meant to join our love as one and bless it from the start.
For fairy love is pure and strong and lasts for endless time,
I thank these fragrant fairy wings for gifts of love sublime.*

Fairy Healing for a Broken Heart

With love comes joy—and sometimes a broken heart. And, just like us, fairies feel love, but don't always mourn its loss the same way we do. Fairies have the unique ability to help heal that weeping wound in so many ways:

- They are of Nature, and Nature is the greatest healer of all . . . take a walk, sit in the park, visit the ocean . . . go where you can. Buy yourself a flower bouquet filled with Flower Fairies and their joy and inhale deeply. Give something back to Nature, which nurtures you.

- They are of the moment, not dwelling in the past or worrying about the future. Be mindful and grateful of all you have right now.

- They are sparkle and joy, an instant mood lifter—they'll do (almost) anything for a laugh.

- They are companionship. Look carefully—you're not alone.

- They are wonder and love. Let yourself feel something good, even if just for a moment.

- They are hope, like the twinkling stars in the sky, they never fade.

When ready to call on your fairy healers, say quietly or aloud:

O fairy love beyond the realm that sees within my heart,
please shine your healing light on me, that darkness may depart.
Replace the numbness in my soul with hope to soothe the pain.
A kiss of fairy wings to let me know you're by my side,
will give me courage to face the world and love myself again.

Fairy Tea Ritual and Spell

A fairy tea can be your chance to go all-out with fairy fun and invite friends and kids to immerse themselves in the world of the fae. There are numerous ideas online and in books for you to indulge your inner fairy goddess with herbs, flowers, sparkle, gossamer wings and other fairy garb, fairy crowns, petite bites, fairy beverages, unicorn treats, and anything else your fairy inspiration can create.

Here, though, we'll focus on a private tea and chat to boost your inner joy and lift your spirits into the Fairy Realm, to refresh your spirit and renew your outlook, so everywhere you look, you see the glow of fairy love—fairy crown and fairy wings optional!

Choose one of the tea recipes following to make or create your own. Fairy tea can really be any hot or cold drink you enjoy—just be sure to make enough for two cups: one for you and one for your fairy guest.

When ready, sit quietly, gently breathe in the aroma of your tea, open your mind and heart to the joy the fairies bring, and say quietly of aloud:

Please, fairy friend, do sit a bit; I am so glad you're here,
to sip and chat and have a laugh like good friends ought to do.
I offer tea I brewed for you to show how much I care,
and eagerly await your sparkling smile, a joy so rare.
This time we spend together is a chance to spread my wings,
to peek into the fairy world and feel the love it brings.

FAIRY'S FAVORITE TEA

Simple, fragrant, and soothing, all you need is water, a lemon, and some of your favorite honey. A splash of whiskey for adults only will appeal to many a fairy, too.

1 Boil 2 cups (480 ml) of water in a kettle.

2 While the water boils, in each of two teacups, stir together 1 tablespoon (20 g) of honey and 1 tablespoon (15 ml) of freshly squeezed lemon juice.

3 Place 1 thin lemon slice in each cup and fill the cups with hot water. Stir, taste, add more lemon juice or honey to taste—and a splash of whiskey, if you please—sit back, and relax.

Fairy Flower Tea

A little more special, this tea is made with dried fairy flowers—hibiscus to enhance intuition and rose for love—and sweetened with vanilla and honey. Be sure to acknowledge the Flower Fairies for their contributions here.

1 Boil 3 cups (720 ml) of water in a small saucepan.

2 Add 3 tablespoons (45 ml) dried food-grade hibiscus flowers, 2 tablespoons (30 ml) dried food-grade rose petals, rose hips, or rose buds, 1/2 vanilla bean, scraped into the water. Let steep for 20 to 30 minutes, or until cooled.

3 Strain the tea through a fine-mesh sieve into a pitcher and discard the solids. Taste and sweeten with honey, as desired.

4 Serve at room temperature or over ice for a refreshing spa-like treat.

PROTECTION AND COURAGE

Fairy Watch and Protection

Often, we're told to beware of the fairies who wish to harm us. But fairies are faithful, protective creatures, too—even the gruff ones can serve as a deterrent to further negative energies surrounding you. When you feel a bit uneasy, or just in general need of protection from what may harm, call on your fairy friends.

Cast a circle using flower petals, fairy dust (see pages 112 and 128), your imagination, fairy lights, candles, or whatever speaks to you. The purpose here is not to set up a barrier, but to define a safe space where the fae are welcome to join you.

Seek the company of any Good Neighbors willing to volunteer their time to look after you. Ask them to stay with you, night and day, until you feel safe. Take a moment to focus on your fears and what the fae can do to help you feel safe. When you're ready, say quietly or aloud:

Join me fairy friends, for in this circle cast, I seek protection from
unknowns of present and of past.
I ask your help to keep me safe from that which means to harm,
to guide and watch and stay alert, to banish any storm.
The lightness of your ways, I pray, to counter any gloom,
that fairy dust and sparkling breeze dispense with pending doom.
My faith and trust I pledge to you, and with gratitude abide—
this sacred pact we make today, my fears are cast aside.

Storm Fairy Magic

In addition to the weather bringing us thunderstorms to get our attention and clear the air, life can conjure pop-up storms along the way that require our courage to sit out, embrace, or navigate. Here, we'll harness the power of the Thunderstorm Fairies, those air elementals who control the weather with their changing moods and intentions. Rainwater, touched by the fairies and gathered during a thunderstorm carries the fairies' powerful courage to bring—and accept—change and protect against harm. The next time a storm is predicted, well before it starts, place a container outside to collect the water—you don't need a lot. When it's safe to retrieve it, bring the water inside. Place an all-seeing tiger's eye crystal in the water and place it on your fairy altar. Spend a moment imbuing the water and the tiger's eye with your intention for courage. When ready to call on the Storm Fairies to assist, say quietly or aloud:

I honor the fairy who brings change so fierce
the winds may hide in fear.
I call on the fairy whose spirit is grace expressed as angry tears.
I ask of the fairy whose sight can see beyond stormy clouds,
to show me courage to brace for what may come,
that I will not be bowed,
but rise and greet the storms of life with strength and will avowed.

Banish Evil Energies

Fairies hate stress of any kind, and are the perfect foil for it when negativity tries to invade your magical space. Take a deep, cleansing breath, in and out, to clear your stressful mind. Imagine the peace you seek, then say quietly or aloud:

For stress be banished here this day, I call on fairy charms,
to calm the winds, soothe the seas, and clear the clouds that harm.
Some fairy dust to cleanse the air and sweet scents to delight,
restore my world to balanced calm, bid evil do take flight.

Invisible Advantage

Being invisible has its advantages—and fairies possess the power of invisibility, being unable to be detected by most humans' sense of sight. This can give fairies the upper hand when they want to just hang out to gather information, hide when they're feeling threatened, retreat to a peaceful place to avoid recognition or stress, or even surprise us by revealing themselves unexpectedly—although most humans won't recognize (read: believe!) what they're seeing! Some fairies will also give charms to humans to make them invisible, so the power *could* be yours for the asking.

To boost your chances of success, seek your own fairy charm to use with this spell—fern seeds. Because of a fern's seemingly mysterious propagation—fern produces neither flower nor seed—it was once believed that the seeds of a fern must be invisible. As a result, legend tells that anyone carrying fern seeds in their pocket will also be invisible! And (logically?) that invisible seed must be born of the invisible flower, which is said to bloom but once a year at midnight on the summer solstice—the best time to gather this fairy charm. (Should you spy the fae out collecting these powerful seeds, too, my advice is to give them first choice and take only what they leave behind.)

Before you begin, spend some time considering what good you would use your invisible strength to achieve. If you've gathered your fern seed and you're ready to ask for the power, say quietly or aloud:

Of secrets from the Fairy Realm, I wish to learn the way
to be unspotted, be unseen, by humans and the fae.
Instead of fairy dust, I sprinkle fern's wee magic seed
that with this charming fairy spell my wish comes true indeed!

Fairy Confidence

Fairies are skilled beings and generally know who they are, what they want, how to get it, and just what to do in almost any situation. They exude a confidence we all wish to emulate, and their confident energies can give support when we need it most. Yellow, the color of confidence, blooms profusely among the Nature fairies, who may just be your best allies when the cry for confidence goes out. Call on any of the Flower Fairies who wear yellow: daisy, buttercup, lily, forsythia, rose, sunflower, pansy, or black-eyed Susan, for starters. Or call on the Tree Fairies, especially in fall when they don their yellow coats: sugar maple, witch hazel, American elm, beech, chestnut, and hickory to name a few. Seek their company when you feel your confidence waning. Light a yellow candle, wear some yellow crystals, then sit quietly and imagine the confident persona you seek to inhabit. When ready, say quietly or aloud:

Among the Nature fairies whose confidence blooms free,
I seek a kindred energy to blossom into me.
The chanting of this spell does signal openness to hear,
just what to do to channel strength and how to banish fear.
And walking with the fairies also signals to the world
that my true self is honored, fairy love it does restore.

Our journey here together, has come upon an end,
but travel on without me now, for you've made fairy friends.

I hope you've seen within your heart a magic thing or two,
and spotted fairy dust—and even spied a fairy, too.

These tales here told require nothing other than belief,
to manifest within your life the magic that you seek.

Enchantment lies in every realm; sometimes, though, you must try
to see beyond the obvious—to look with your third eye.

You're ready now to greet the fae, on terms that are your own,
to cast a fairy magic spell, to walk the path alone.

Though near I'll stay to cheer you on, to keep you safe from harm,
to scatter fairy dust to guide and sprinkle fairy charm.

Please close your eyes and take some time to honor fairy friends,
for lessons reaped and magic steeped in wonder without end.

RESOURCES AND REFERENCES

Ancient Origins—Reconstructing the Origins of Humanity's Past: Ancient-Origins.net.

Ancient-Symbols.com.

Barker, Cicely Mary. *The Complete Book of the Flower Fairies*. New York: Frederick Warne (Penguin Random House LLC), 2019 (first U.S. edition).

Briggs, Katharine. *An Encyclopedia of Fairies: Hobgoblins, Brownies, Bogies, and Other Supernatural Creatures*. New York: Pantheon (Random House), 1976 (first American edition).

British Fairies: BritishFairies.wordpress.com.

Daimler, Morgan. "Introduction to Faery and Celtic Witchcraft." ToSalem.com.

Enchanted Living magazine: EnchantedLivingMag.com.

Encyclopaedia Britannica: Britannica.com.

Encyclopedia.com. "Wee Folk and Their Friends." Encyclopedia.com/science/encyclopedias-almanacs-transcripts-and-maps/wee-folk-and-their-friends.

How Stuff Works—History: "Who Is the Sandman?": https://history.howstuffworks.com/history-vs-myth/who-is-sandman.htm.

Grove and Grotto: GroveandGrotto.com.

Guiley, Rosemary Ellen. *Fairy Magic*. London: Element (HarperCollins Publishers), 2004.

Guiley, Rosemary Ellen. *The Encyclopedia of Magic and Alchemy*. Milford, CT: Visionary Living, Inc., 2006.

Historic UK: Historic-UK.com.

Irish Music Daily: IrishMusicDaily.com/danny-boy-history.

Learn Religions: learnreligions.com.

LiveScience.com.

Melville, Francis. *The Book of Faeries*. London: Quarto Inc., 2002.

Mythology.net.

Mythopedia: Mythopedia.com.

National Day Calendar: NationalDayCalendar.com.

National Leprechaun Museum: LeprechaunMuseum.ie.

Native American Legends: Native-Languages.org.

Occult World: OccultWorld.com.

O'Conor, Norreys Jephson. "The Early Irish Fairies and Fairyland." *The Sewanee Review* 28, no. 4 (October 1920): 545–557. The Johns Hopkins University Press. jstor.org/stable/27533351.

Oman, C. C. "The English Folklore of Gervase of Tilbury." *Folklore* 55, no. 1 (1944): 2–15. Accessed June 27, 2021. www.jstor.org/stable/1257623.

Pūkui, Mary Kawena (compiler), Caroline Curtis (reteller), Robin Burningham (illustrator). *Tales of the Menehune*, revised edition. Copyright 1960; 1985, Kamehameha Schools Press, Honolulu, HI. ULUKAU: The Hawaiian Electronic Library.

Royal Museums Greenwich: RMG.co.uk/.

Sacred-Texts.com.

Spirit Walk Ministry: SpiritWalkMinistry.com.

Springwolf, D. D., PhD. "The Magikal Faery Spirits of Nature." Springwolf. net/2015/07/18/faeries-pixies-and-sprites/.

Springwolf, D. D., PhD. *The Pagan's Path*. PagansPath.com.

Sweden.org.

Tea and Rosemary (blog): TeaandRosemary.com.

Telesco, Patricia. "Fairy Magic: Devas, Elementals, and Other Magical Spirits—Wise Witches and Witchcraft." WitchcraftandWitches.com.

Theoi Project: Theoi.com.

Tooth Fairy Rate: prnewswire.com/news-releases/tooth-fairy-payouts-plunge-for-second-consecutive-year-300798356.html.

Wells, Rosemary. "The Making of an Icon: The Tooth Fairy in North American Folklore and Popular Culture." in *The Good People: New Fairylore Essays*, New York: Garland, 1991.

World History Encyclopedia: WorldHistory.org.

Yale University, Human Relations Area Files: Luck of the Irish: https://hraf.yale.edu/luck-of-the-irish-folklore-and-fairies-in-rural-ireland/.

INDEX

A

acquaintance, 33
  elementals, 42–65
  household/helper fairies,
    66–71
  offerings, 34–37
  other fairies, 72–82
  Tuatha Dé Danann, 38–40
air fairies, 42
altar, 101–4
Alux, 17
Alven, 17
amethyst, 105
angel aura crystal, 105
aquamarine, 105
Asrai, 47
Aziza, 48

B

babies, 150
Ballybog, 72–73
Banshee, 17, 73
belief
  Fairy Realm, 26–28
  magical powers, 20–23
  malevolent fairies, 24–25
  origins, 13–15
  primer, 16–19
  spirit guides, 29–31
blooms, 147–48
Boggart, 17
Bogle, 17
Brownie, 17, 67

C

career change, 141
celestite, 106
Chaneque, 17
Changeling, 17
changelings, 74
Chin Chin Kobakama, 67
citrine, 106
clair senses, 87
Clurichaun, 17, 74
communication, 85
  etiquette, 86–87
  gardens, 94–99
  tools, 100–118
    working with fairies,
    88–93
confidence, 170
crystals, 105–9

D

dandelion, 113, 154–55
Danu, 40
Deva, 17, 48
Domovoi, 68
Dryad, 17, 49
Duende, 17
Dwarf, 17, 50–51

E

earth fairies, 43–44
elder tree, 113
elementals, 42–45
Elf, 17, 51
enchantment
  festivities, 120–25
  meditation, 132–37
  potions, 126–31
  spells/rituals, 138–70
Esbat, 125
Esprit Follet, 18

F

fairies, 10–11, 13
  befriending, 33–83
  belief in, 13–31
  classes of, 46
  communicating with,
    85–117
  contacting, 157
  magic of, 119–70
  magical powers of, 20–23
  malevolence of, 24–25
  origins of, 14–15
  realm of, 26–28
  as spirit guides, 29–31
  types, 16–19
fairy dust, 98–99, 112, 128–31
Fairy Godmother, 75
fairy quartz, 106
Fairy Realm, 26–28
fairy star, 110–11
fairy stones, 109–10
festivities, 120–25
fire fairies, 43
firefly fairy freedom, 142
Flower Fairy, 52
found things, 117
foxglove, 114
friendship, 140
  offerings of, 34–36

G

gardens, planning, 94–99
Geoffrey of Monmouth, 14
Gervase of Tilbury, 14
Gillie Dhu, 64
Gnom, 18
Gnome, 53
Goblin, 18, 76
green jade, 106

H

hawthorn tree, 37
home
  finding, 145
  selling, 146
honeysuckle, 114
house fairies, 66–71
herbs, 113–15
Huldra, 64

I

inner peace, 152
International Fairy Day, 16
intuition, 156
intuitive senses, 86
Irish sea water guardian, 18

J

journaling, 89–90

K

Kelpie, 18
Knockers, 18
Kobold, 18
Kodama, 64

L

Lady of the Lake, 54–55
lady's mantle, 115
Leprechaun, 18, 76–77
Leshy, 64
luck, 142

M

Mazzamurello, 69
meditation, 91, 93, 132–37
Menehune, 55
Merfolk, 18, 56–57
midnight, 23
Midsummer's Night Dream, A
(Shakespeare), 14
moldavite, 107
Monaciello, 69
Moon, phases of, 125
Moss People, 64

N

nature fairies, 45
new horizons, 144
new intentions, 143
Nisse, 18
Nymph, 18, 58–59

P

Peri, 19, 77
pets, 152–53
Pixie, 19, 77
Pooka, 19
potions, 126–31
prehnite, 107

R

rainbow aura quartz, 107
rainbow moonstone, 108
Redcap, 19
rituals
    abundance and success,
      139–43
    communication, 156–58
    everyday living, 144–55
    love and joy, 159–65
    protection and courage,
      166–70
Robin Goodfellow, 78
rose quartz, 108

S

Sabbats, 120–24
Salamander, 19, 59
Seelie Court, 19, 78–79
Selkie, 19, 60
sleep, 149
spells. See rituals
Sprite, 19, 61
summer solstice, 99
Sylph, 19, 62

T

Tomte, 70–71
tools, 100–118
Tooth Fairy, 80
tourmaline, 108–9
Trasgu, 71
Tree Spirit, 63
truth, 158
Tuatha Dé Danann, 15, 38–39
turquoise, 109

U

Undine, 65
Unseelie Court, 19, 81

V

vervain, 115

W

wand, 112
water, 127
water fairies, 44
wealth, growing, 139
well-being, 150–51
Will-O'-the-Wisp, 19
Will-o'-the-Wisp, 82
wings, 116
wishes, 116
witches, 138

Y

Yaksha, 19
Yosei, 19

Z

Zashiki Warashi, 7

Acknowledgments

A true bit of fairy magic goes into each book made and thanks are due to many for it. The portal to this magical world was opened for me by Quarto Publisher, Rage Kindelsperger. Thank you. May the fairies bless you with unending joy and creativity in return.

My editors—Leeann Moreau, guided the process with sparkle and a bit of fairy wisdom along the way, and for the fairy dust trail she leaves in its wake, I'm grateful. Cara Donaldson exhibited true fairy calm and charm through the final phases of manuscript development and expertly guided the book through production where it was transformed into the best version of itself. Her graceful elegance leaves a beautiful mark on this world, including this book you hold in your hand. May the fairies grant your dearest wish. Elizabeth You joined the fairy troop during the final dance and didn't miss a beat! And to the rest of the Quarto teams, my sincere thanks for all you do to create and sell such beautiful books.

To my husband, John, my dearest treasure, thank you for your unfailing ability to see magic everywhere, and for sharing that vision with me. Your love and trust are truly inspiring, and you bring me joy unending each day.

To all my friends and family who cast magic into my life daily, thank you for your love and support.